Gobbledygook

A Dictionary That's ⅔ Accurate, ⅓ Nonsense—and 100% Up to You to Decide

WILLIAM WILSON

Adams media
Avon, Massachusetts

Dedication / Acknowledgments

I would like to acknowledge students at High Point Central High School for coming up with a handful of the nonsense words. Thanks to Peter Archer for supplying some of the odd "real" words. I would like to dedicate this book to my family: my wife, Tiffany; my son, Parker-John; my stepson, Jake; and my stepdaughter, Abigail. I would also like to thank Justin Cord Hayes, *sine qua non*.

Copyright © 2011 by F+W Media, Inc.
All rights reserved.
This book, or parts thereof, may not be reproduced in any
form without permission from the publisher; exceptions are
made for brief excerpts used in published reviews.

Published by
Adams Media, a division of F+W Media, Inc.
57 Littlefield Street, Avon, MA 02322. U.S.A.
www.adamsmedia.com

ISBN 10: 1-4405-2818-7
ISBN 13: 978-1-4405-2818-7
eISBN 10: 1-4405-2924-8
eISBN 13: 978-1-4405-2924-5

Printed in the United States of America.

10   9   8   7   6   5   4   3   2   1

Library of Congress Cataloging-in-Publication Data
is available from the publisher.

This publication is designed to provide accurate and authoritative information with regard to the subject matter covered. It is sold with the understanding that the publisher is not engaged in rendering legal, accounting, or other professional advice. If legal advice or other expert assistance is required, the services of a competent professional person should be sought.
　　—From a *Declaration of Principles* jointly adopted by a Committee of the American Bar Association and a Committee of Publishers and Associations

Many of the designations used by manufacturers and sellers to distinguish their product are claimed as trademarks. Where those designations appear in this book and Adams Media was aware of a trademark claim, the designations have been printed with initial capital letters.

This book is available at quantity discounts for bulk purchases.
For information, please call 1-800-289-0963.

Introduction

So, you think you're King Wordsmith, do you? Well, Your Highness, this book will put you to the test.

I've sailed the sea of words that comprise the English language and have returned with a fine catch of little-known, obscure, archaic, outdated, and idiosyncratic terms and expressions. And I'm willing to bet that among them are more than a few that will make that crown rest uneasily on your brow.

Ready? Open the book and thumb through it. On each right-hand page you'll find three words. Two of them are obscure, but legitimate, words you would find in an unabridged dictionary (*very* unabridged). One of them, however, is a neologism . . . better known as a fake word, made up to fool you. It's up to you to figure out which is real—and which is false.

What follows then is a sophisticated game for the intellectually aspiring. You can play by yourself while sipping a glass of ice-cold sherry and nibbling on shrimp in a garlic-butter sauce.

Or you can challenge your guests at your next dinner party, as all of you roll your favorite varietal gently on your palate and pass around the walnuts and Brie.

In teams (if there is an abundance of you) or individually (if but a few), read the words aloud—a handy pronunciation guide is included with each word—along with their parts of speech and their definitions. See if your opponent(s)—or you—can guess the fake word. If they do, then give them a point. Perhaps you can go for, say, best of ten or best of twenty, or just see who gets to a certain number first.

In addition to the words themselves, I've filled *Gobbledygook* chock-full of trivia related—sometimes directly and sometimes *very* tangentially—to many of the words. If you've played this game by yourself, then you can impress your friends with your "trivial" knowledge, which should get you invited to a lot more cocktail parties or at least to the types of parties where people like talking about words and playing word games. Be prepared to turn to one of your fellow guests and say, casually, "Are you aware that xarque (pronounced SHAR-kay) is a Portuguese form of beef jerky? Or, perhaps, not." Then smile mysteriously and glide off to the bar for another white wine.

Good luck!

ab absurdo, capacitance, bibliometagraphia

1. **ab absurdo (ab-uhb-SIR-doh) (adv. or adj.):** An argument or statement that is false because it is patently absurd. The next time you think someone is full of it, *cry ab absurdo!* Democrats won't raise taxes? Ab absurdo! Republicans really care about people without money? Ab absurdo!

2. **capacitance (kuh-PASS-uh-tuhnts) (noun):** The property of an electric nonconductor permitting energy storage as the result of electric displacement when opposite surfaces of the nonconductor are maintained at a difference of potential. The inverse of capacitance is called elastance.

3. **bibliometagraphia (bib-lee-oh-met-uh-GRAPH-ee-uh) (noun):** Data compiling the length of a string of words a person has read, based on page count, book size, and other factors. The word's roots are Greek: *biblion* (book); –graphos (to write). Libraries use this data to make decisions about purchases; determining, for example, if a book should be in the circulating or in the reference library.

The fake word is:
bibliometagraphia

Although you might think it would be useful for libraries to have some idea of how many words the average reader goes through in a given year, there's no such word as BIBLIOMETAGRAPHIA. Libraries make decisions about whether a book should circulate based on the condition and rarity of the book, its cost to the library, how often it's consulted by users, and other factors. Sadly, though, how many words the average reader reads isn't one of the metrics in deciding this.

Speedy Reader

Howard Stephen Berg claims the record for the fastest reader in the world. According to *Guinness Book of World Records*, Berg clocks in at 80 pages or approximately 25,000 words per minute. However, he admits that at this speed he only gets the general concepts and not the details of what he reads. In a televised test, however, Berg only managed about 30 pages or 5,500 words a minute. Still, even at that reduced pace, Berg would be able to speed-read the King James Bible (783,137 words) in about 142 minutes—or two-and-a-half hours.

---

delatynite, scrapulous, humuhumunukunukuapuaa

1. **delatynite (duh-LAT-uh-night) (noun):** Sulfur-lacking amber, high in carbon, found at Delatyn in the Carpathian mountains of Galicia. Galicia, for those of you who are a bit shaky on geography, is part of the Ukraine. The town of Delatyn was at various points passed back and forth between Poland, the Austro-Hungarian Empire, and the Soviet Union.

2. **scrapulous (SCRAP-yuh-luss) (adj.):** Coming from an Old Norse root meaning "scrape," scrapulous describes jagged and uneven surfaces likely to cause injury to the unsuspecting. The word was first used by James Boswell in his *Journal of a Tour to the Hebrides*: "Outside Dundee we climbed a small mountainside, Dr. Johnson commenting much upon the scrapulous character of the rocks."

3. **humuhumunukunukuapuaa (hyoom-uh-HYOOM-uh-nyook-uh-nyook-uh-ahp-uh-wah-ah) (noun):** A small Hawaiian triggerfish. Native islanders joke that the pig-nosed, colorful fish's name is much longer than the fish itself. *Nuku* is the Hawaiian word for "nose," and repeating it makes the nose smaller.

The fake word is:
scrapulous

Words such as "scrape" do, in fact, come from an Old Norse word, *skrapa*, meaning "to scrape." SCRAPULOUS also could be related to the Latin *scrobis*, meaning trench, and even to the Russian *skorb*, meaning sorrow, grief. In sorrow, though, I must tell you that there's no such word as SCRAPULOUS.

Little Fish, Big Name

You might think that humuhumunukunukuapuaa is the longest fish name in Hawaiian, but that's not the case. The lauwiliwilinukunuku'oi'oiv, whose name means "long-snouted fish shaped like a wiliwili leaf," holds that distinction. The humuhumunukunukuapuaa can claim an even greater distinction, however. The brightly colored swimmer with the pig-like snout is the state fish of Hawaii, and it is mentioned in the classic island tune, "My Little Grass Shack in Kealakekua, Hawaii." More recently, it was featured in a scene in the Russell Brand comedy, *Forgetting Sarah Marshall*. Dwayne the bartender gives this classic reply to the question, "What's the state fish of Hawaii?": "The humuhumunukunukuapuaa. Yeah, bitch!"

---

chremsel, Wieshastation, faciation

1. **chremsel (KREM-ZULL) (noun)**: A flat fried cake made with matzoh meal eaten at Passover. Other Passover treats that may sound unusual to Gentile ears include beitzah (a roasted egg symbolizing continued existence), zeroah (a piece of roasted lamb shankbone symbolizing sacrificial offerings), and charoset (a mixture of apple, nuts, wine, and cinnamon, calling to mind the mortar Jews used to construct buildings during slavery times).

2. **Wieshastation (WEEZ-hass-stay-shun) (noun, usually capitalized)**: The process of eliminating two or more factors from a mathematical equation in order to simplify the equation, named for German scientist Gerhard Wiehaste. This method is used most often by geologists and archaeologists.

3. **faciation (fay-she-AY-shun) (noun)**: An ecological association's subdivision characterized by the codominance of two or more forms of the association, constituting a community of considerable extent, its area often related to a climactic variation within the area of association. According to lovers of nature's mind-altering herb, faciation does not create particularly good marijuana plants.

The fake word is:

Wieshastation

One can, in some cases, "streamline" a mathematical equation by simplifying radicals. A radical is an alternate way to write an exponential whose exponent is a reciprocal. A radical is in its simplest form if it has been reduced as much as possible or if there are no radicals in the denominator. "Wie haste" is German for "How did?"

Don't "Passover" This Treat

Here's a chremsel recipe from Beth Israel Congregation in Bath, Maine (courtesy of Marjorie Milkes).

1 cup matzoh meal
1 cup water or soup or wine
1 tablespoon chopped almonds (optional)
1 teaspoon sugar (optional)
¼ teaspoon salt
4 eggs, separated

1. Sift meal into bowl. Bring liquid to the boiling point, then stir into meal.

2. Add almonds, sugar, salt, and beaten egg yolks. Lastly, add stiffly beaten egg whites to the mixture.

3. Drop by tablespoon into a little oil in skillet (or can be deep fried in oil heated to 375°). Fry until brown. Drain on paper towel.

4. Sprinkle with powdered sugar (optional) or serve with sour cream and jelly or cinnamon and sugar.

Faliscan, Palembang, fraternite

1. **Faliscan (fuh-LISS-kin) (adj., usually capitalized):** Relating to the Falisci who inhabited the city of Falerii and its region in ancient Etruria, it also refers to the language used by these people. The Falisci resisted Rome's dominance until about 396 b.c., rebelled in 358 b.c., and tried a final time to gain independence from Rome during the First Punic War. The Falisci finally gave up around 241 b.c.

2. **Palembang (PALL-uhm-bahn) (adj., usually capitalized):** Of or from the city of Palembang, Indonesia, in Sumatra and related to the style common there. Palembang once was capital of the ancient Buddhist kingdom of Srivijaya, which controlled large sections of present-day Indonesia, Malaysia, and southern Thailand.

3. **fraternite (fruh-TERN-ite) (noun):** A mineral discovered in 1948 by students at the University of Texas, Austin. It is characterized by a silvery color and naturally occurring low-grade radiation. Fraternitite once was a key component of quartz watches.

The fake word is:
fraternite

A fraternity has not discovered any minerals, but there is a "Fraternity Rock" in New Jersey at which a mineral was discovered. Better known as "Snake Hill" or "Laurel Hill," some call this large, stone formation in Secaucus "Fraternity Rock" because fraternities in the area paint their Greek letters on it. The mineral "Petersite" was discovered there in 1981 by Nicholas Facciolla and named for Thomas A. and Joseph Peters, curators of a natural history museum in Paterson, New Jersey.

Faliscan, You're Dead!

The Faliscan language never had a chance. First, it was co-opted by the more-popular, now-also-dead language, Latin, both of which emanated from the Italian peninsula. Most likely, Faliscan survived as a distinct language until about 150 B.C. About 355 Faliscan inscriptions survive, including this one from a drinking vessel: *foied vino pipafo, cra carefo.* In other words, "I will drink wine; tomorrow, I won't have any." Pretty good advice if you ask me.

---

fromaddio, phthirius, drumble-drone

1. **fromaddio (froh-MAH-dee-oh) (adv. or adj.):** A musical term, indicating that a piece should be played at half-speed for exactly four bars. English composer Gustav Holst—best known for his orchestral suite *The Planets*—frequently wrote music that contained this musical direction.

2. **phthirius (THEER-ee-us) (noun):** A genus containing the crab louse. Yes, this is the little critter most people claim they picked up from a toilet seat. However, they don't just ingratiate themselves with one's genitals; they also can find comfy homes in one's hair and eyelashes.

3. **drumble-drone (DRUM-bull-DRONE) (noun):** A drone bee or a stupid and useless person. "Devonshire Children's Song," composed by British poet Oliver Madox Brown (1855–1874), focuses on the busy bee's trip in an apple orchard. Brown was son of the famed English painter Ford Madox Brown, perhaps best known for his painting *The Last of England*, which depicts British emigrants heading for a new life away from the mother country.

The fake word is:
fromaddio

Consequently, Holst's *The Planets* doesn't contain this tempo, but it does contain the extremely rare musical direction "ffff." In music, "f" means "forte," or loud, and "ff" means fortissimo, or very loud. Holst brings the noise even more in both the "Mars" and "Uranus" sections of his orchestral suite, which tell the musician to play "ffff." Gustav Mahler has Holst beat, however. Mahler's *Seventh Symphony* adds yet another "f," but the sire of strident surely is Romanian composer Gyorgy Ligeti, whose "The Devil's Staircase" progresses at one point from fffff to fffffff (!!). Who says only rock is played at ear-splitting levels?

Now, That's Italian

Don't know your allegretto (a little bit joyful) from your tenuto (sustained)? For that matter, do you wonder why so many musical terms are in Italian? The answer is the Renaissance. While most of us associate this fecund period with the visual arts, it also was a fertile time for music. The best music schools in the world could be found in Italy. Budding composers, who began to experiment with all sorts of tempos while studying there, wrote their directions in the local language then took their compositions back home. As a result, Italian notation began to dominate music, as it does to this day.

---

brangle, chrysemys, fringle

1. **brangle (BRAHN-gull) (noun):** A blend of "brawl" and "wrangle," which is a synonym for "squabble." Brangles erupt whenever people get together to discuss sports, politics, or religion.

2. **chrysemys (KRISS-uh-muss) (noun):** A small, brightly marked freshwater turtle found in North America. The so-called "painted turtle" is the only species of the *Chrysemys* genus.

3. **fringle (FREENG-uhl) (verb):** To exchange goods and services for artistic work, be it painting, writing, sculpting, etc. One of the most significant fringles of all time occurred when a young Picasso traded some early black and white sketches for a month's rent. Later, this early Picasso patron sold the sketches for hundreds of thousands of dollars.

The fake word is:
fringle

Picasso experienced extreme poverty when he first moved to France from Spain, but he achieved fame pretty quickly. While still in his early twenties, he was championed by Gertrude Stein and other members of her family. The Steins had a good eye for art. They also championed the young Henri Matisse, who became a lifelong friend and rival of Picasso. The two met at Gertrude Stein's place. Her collection of the works of struggling artists are, indeed, now priceless.

Turtle Trivia

The painted turtle (*Chrysemys picta*) is the most widely distributed turtle in North America; it resides in freshwater ponds, lakes, marshes, and creeks from Canada to Louisiana. Painted turtles are not genetically male or female. Gender is determined by outside temperature during embryogenesis. *Chrysemys picta* can live up to forty years in the wild, while your average hare or rabbit only lives between five and ten years. Talk about the tortoise beating the hare!

ungrute, scyphus, tralatitious

1. **ungrute** (UHN-groot) (noun): A small, mountainous shrub, found in portions of the American Southwest. Desert bighorn sheep, Nevada's state animal, consider ungrute a delicacy and, in times of extreme drought, can decimate this shrub nearly to extinction.

2. **scyphus** (SIGH-fuzz) (noun): A drinking vessel common in ancient Greece. It contained a deep body, flat bottom, and two small handles near the rim. Scyphus, Ltd., a British company, makes "quality disposable paper cups" featuring "state of the art" production.

3. **tralatitious** (TRAL-uh-tish-us) (adj.): Possessing significance from an extraneous source; or, handed down, as from one generation to another. Thus, "traditional morality" or "traditional knowledge" are tralatitious concepts.

The fake word is:
ungrute

While desert bighorn sheep do consider various grasses and shrubs delicacies, they cannot nosh on ungrute because no such shrub exists. If it did exist, desert bighorn sheep would be able get nourishment from ungrute because the sheep have a sophisticated, nine-stage digestive process. Consequently, bighorns can get nutrients out of practically any food source. Male bighorns need their sustenance because they love to engage in head-butting; these macho displays can last as many as twenty-four hours!

Political Morality?!?

While you would be forgiven for believing the words "political" and "morality" cannot coexist, learned folks such as Jonathan Haidt, a professor at the University of Virginia, focuses on the psychological basis of morality in political ideologies. He has found that people who consider themselves liberals value caring and fairness more than loyalty, respect, and purity. Self-professed conservatives, on the other hand, place greater value on loyalty, respect, and purity than on caring and fairness. Why? According to Haidt, it's because conservative ideologies were born in tight-knit, homogeneous societies, while liberal ideologies sprang from cities, which typically contain greater cultural diversity.

---

grimthorpe, zifgrind, iconodule

1. **grimthorpe** (GRIM-thorp) (verb): To remodel an ancient building without the knowledge or care to keep its original quality and character intact, named for Sir Edmund Beckett, first Baron Grimthorpe, who died in 1905 after (some say) totally bungling the restoration of England's St. Albans Cathedral.

2. **zifgrind** (ZIFF-grinned) (noun): A hypothesis based on knowledge of ancient texts. Zifgrinds have been responsible for some of the "knowledge" about UFOs and their connection to ancient cultures.

3. **iconodule** (eye-KAHN-uh-dyool) (noun): One who reveres or worships icons and defends their use as devotional objects. Iconodules are the opposite of iconoclasts, those who seek to break with traditional conventions or dogma.

The fake word is:
zifgrind

Plenty of scholars, philosophers, and everyday people base their knowledge on ancient texts, especially spiritual ones, but the word zifgrind doesn't exist. Sometimes, this knowledge can have more than spiritual consequences. In India, for example, ancient texts are being used to improve modern-day agriculture. The Centre for Indian Knowledge Systems, a think tank devoted to connecting ancient texts to modern-day issues, works with farmers throughout India reviving traditional farming practices gleaned from Vrkshayurveda, an ancient Indian text. By doing so, they have developed "new" rice and vegetable varieties that are protected by ancient forms of pest control.

We Were Not Alone

Swiss author Erich von Daniken achieved his fifteen minutes of fame in the late 1960s-early 1970s with his book *Chariots of the Gods?* The book's hypothesis is that ancient cultures achieved incredible leaps in knowledge thanks to visits from E.T. and his buddies. The Egyptian pyramids? Extraterrestrials. Stonehenge? Extraterrestrials. Bizarre visions of Old Testament prophets? Extraterrestrials. Need proof? Well, you can start with the so-called Piri Reis map, an Ottoman-Turkish map that appears to depict portions of Earth from space. Still not convinced? Then consider Peru's Nazca Lines. The lines, carved into rocky terrain, create pictures so large that their designs—monkeys, spiders, lizards—can only be appreciated from an airplane or some other identified flying object.

ochronosis, stultiloquence, flangyphygosis

1. **ochronosis (oh-kruh-NO-suss) (noun):** A rarely occurring familial condition characterized by pigment deposits in cartilage, ligaments, and tendons. A common symptom of the condition is bluish-black ear discoloration.

2. **stultiloquence (stull-TILL-uh-kwents) (noun):** Senseless, silly talk. This is a mainstay of the average Twitter account, and it is related to the word "grandiloquence," which refers to long-winded, pompous, or bombastic speech. (At least the limits of Twitter don't allow for too much of that . . .)

3. **flangyphygosis (flan-jee-phy-GO-sis) (noun):** A medical condition marked by swollen appendages, often caused by common office equipment. It is, basically, a less-serious version of carpal tunnel syndrome and one that has become widespread in an age of near-constant texting.

The fake word is:
flangyphygosis

Carpal tunnel syndrome affects the wrist's median nerve, which enters your hand through the so-called carpal tunnel. Typing is probably the main carpal tunnel culprit, but it is not alone. Sewing, driving, painting, use of tools, playing sports (especially racquet sports), and even playing some musical instruments can lead to carpal tunnel syndrome.

— Shut Up Already, Mr. President! —

Warren G. Harding, the nation's 29th president, is best known today—if he is known at all—for three things: Teapot Dome (an early oil scandal), dying while in office, and consistently making the list of worst presidents. But that's not all! In addition to these "accomplishments," Harding is notable for being one of our most grandiloquent presidents. And, boy, could he rock his alliteration, as this quotation suggests: "Progression is not proclamation nor palaver. It is not pretense nor play on prejudice. It is not of personal pronouns nor perennial pronouncement. It is not the perturbation of a people passion-wrought, nor a promise proposed." No wonder it's alleged that Harding died because his wife poisoned him. She probably just wanted him to shut up!

---

tregetour, maranchine, pribble

1. **tregetour (TREDGE-ed-ur) (noun):** A juggler or magician; a sleight-of-hand artist. Chaucer's *House of Fame* includes a reference to "Colle tregetor," a magician gifted enough to hide a windmill under a walnut shell.

2. **maranchine (muh-RANCH-een) (adj.):** Of or related to those who make plans most would consider patently foolish and/or impossible. In both *As You Like It* and *All's Well That Ends Well*, Shakespeare includes "clowns" (basically, comic relief—not folks in clown makeup) described as "maranchine."

3. **pribble (PRIH-bull) (noun):** A minor argument or trivial discussion. Pribbles are pet peeves, not huge problems. Parking ticket? Pribble. Stolen car? Problem.

The fake word is:

maranchine

Shakespeare typically included clowns or fools in his works, and they were performed by, among others, actor William Kempe. Kempe probably originated the role of Falstaff in Shakespeare's two *Henry IV* plays, and the roles of Dogberry (*Much Ado about Nothing*) and Peter (*Romeo and Juliet*) most likely were written with him in mind. *Hamlet* contains a possible clue to Kempe's departure from Shakespeare's theater company, the Lord Chamberlain's Men, in 1599. At one point in Shakespeare's magnum opus, Hamlet complains about clowns who appreciate improvisation too much.

Tregetour Extraordinaire

Alexander Herrmann, also known as Herrmann the Great, may have been the most proficient tregetour in history. The Frenchman made his name in London and later became a naturalized U.S. citizen. At a typical Herrmann show, the magician would produce cards, cards, and more cards seemingly from thin air. Then, he would do rapid-fire sleight-of-hand tricks with them until he moved on to "producing" coins and then making them vanish.

In truth, Herrmann's abracadabra oeuvre wasn't a whole lot different from that of other magicians of his time, but what made him "the Great" was his propensity for showmanship. For example, while other tregetours might settle simply for pulling a rabbit out of a hat, Herrmann would produce a rabbit, throw it out into the air over the audience, pull out a pistol (!!), and shoot at it. The rabbit would disappear, and Herrmann would go into the audience, pulling the probably-quite-frazzled rabbit from the coattails of a spectator. Herrmann died in 1896 in New York of a heart attack at the age of fifty-two.

---

scromlish, noosphere, Uvean

1. **scromlish (SKRAHM-lish) (noun):** A Scottish delicacy consisting of the brains of various regional animals. Scots eat pounds of this stuff every year on St. Flaherty's Day, which commemorates the patron saint of sheep.

2. **noosphere (NO-uh-sfeer) (noun):** The sphere of human perception in regard to its influence on both the biosphere and evolution. The term was introduced by French philosopher Pierre Teilhard de Chardin.

3. **Uvean (you-VAY-uhn) (adj., usually capitalized):** Relating to the people of Uvea. This Polynesian island, confusingly, is also known as the Wallis Islands after its "discoverer," Capt. Samuel Wallis, who also "discovered" Tahiti. In the Uvean language, "Uvea" basically means "main island of the Wallis Islands."

The fake word is:
scromlish

Sheep have not one, but two patron saints, but neither of them are St. Flaherty because there *is* no St. Flaherty. And there is no such Scottish delicacy called scromlish.

St. Drogo was born of Flemish nobility in 1105. His mother died in childbirth, which seems to have caused him no end of guilt. Perhaps to expiate that guilt, Drogo spent the last forty years of his life subsisting on little more than water and the Eucharist (the wafer Roman Catholics eat as part of Mass). In addition to "patronizing" sheep, St. Drogo also is the patron saint of, among other things, gallstones, hernias, and housekeepers.

St. George is the other patron saint of sheep. Drogo's association with sheep is unclear, but there is a connection between George and wooly domestic creatures. The infamous dragon with which George is forever associated subsisted first on mutton, eating two sheep per day. Before long, mutton became so scarce that villages began forcing young maidens to draw lots. "Winners" got eaten by the dragon, of course. Fortunately, St. George came along and saved the day.

Wallis and His *Dolphin*

British sea captain Samuel Wallis became commander of the *Dolphin* in 1766. His mission? To find the other continent believed to exist near South America. Being short on supplies, Wallis instead found Tahiti and Uvea/Wallis on June 18, 1767. Wallis named Tahiti "King George Island" in honor of his contemporary British monarch.

---

preterition, waddy, glistant

1. **preterition (pred-uh-RIH-shun) (noun):** A Calvinistic doctrine that proclaims God has left to eternal death all those He did not, for unknown reasons, choose to give eternal life. The notably dour Calvinist tradition also includes the heart-warming tenet of "total depravity," which states that all people—from little babies to Mother Teresa—are born riddled throughout with sin.

2. **waddy (WAHD-ee) (noun):** A throwing stick Australian Aborigines use in hunting and war. Waddies are also known as "nulla nulla."

3. **glistant (GLISST-unt) (adj.):** A word, coined by Irish poet Sean McIlheney, to describe something that can be glimpsed in the distance. It appears in this line from "Angels at the Ready," which most consider his best-known poem: "And into glistant realms of view / The seraphs dance on unaware."

The fake word is:

glistant

Although Ireland hasn't produced a famous poet named Sean McIlheney, the land of St. Patrick has produced more than its share of literary giants, including Nobel Prize–winning poet William Butler Yeats. Yeats was a master of language, but he mostly avoided neologisms.

Calvinism Isn't Dead

France-born John Calvin wasn't the only theologian to grapple with "reforming" the Roman Catholic Church during the sixteenth century, but his influence was so great that many strains of the Protestant Reformation have come to bear his name. Calvin's brand of spirituality was noticeably bleak.

In addition to "total depravity," Calvinism also includes such doctrines as "limited atonement." Limited atonement does not suggest that Jesus Christ's sacrifice was "limited," only that God chose certain people to save from damnation. Christ's grace only "works" for those elected by God for salvation. If you're not one of the lucky few, then you're going to be burning with Satan in Hell for all eternity.

---

brulyie, squatchy, anestrus

1. **brulyie (BROOL-yee) (noun):** Related to the word "broil," a brulyie is a donnybrook, a row, a scuffle. In other words, it occurs when tempers get to a "broiling" point.

2. **squatchy (SKWAH-chee) (adj.):** Of or relating to pine straw, especially when pine straw is used in cultivated gardens. According to pine straw purveyors, squatchy gardens reduce weeds, moderate soil temperature, and improve soil fertility.

3. **anestrus (an-ES-truss) (noun):** The period of non-sexual activity between periods of sexual activity in cyclically breeding mammals. It is the opposite of the word "estrus." Estrus is also the name of a Washington state-based record label, whose acts include Man or Astro-man?, Fatal Flying Guilloteens, and The Diplomats of Solid Sound.

The fake word is:

squatchy

Would you believe the word squatchy is related to the cryptozoological being known variously as a skunk ape, Bigfoot, or Sasquatch? No? Good. In America, tales of these half-man/half-ape creatures date back to tales told by indigenous Pacific Northwest tribes. The Lummi spoke of *Ts'emekwes*. Other tribes told tales of cannibalistic creatures living on Mount St. Helens.

Sasquatch/Bigfoot sightings exploded in the mid-twentieth century. Footprints appeared, seemingly all over the Northwest, in the 1950s.

A famous film of a Sasquatch came to light in 1967. Roger Patterson and Robert Gimlin supposedly caught Bigfoot on tape, taking a stroll through Bluff Creek, California. The video was shown on various mysterious phenomena shows for decades to come. Eventually, an acquaintance of Patterson claimed he was the man in the Sasquatch suit.

The Washington Scene

Estrus is not the only independent music label to thrive in Washington. Other labels include Green Monkey Records (The Icons, Tom Dyer), K Records (Adrian Orange, label founder Calvin Johnson), and, of course, Sub Pop Records, which will forever be associated with the so-called grunge movement of the 1990s. Before achieving international prominence, Nirvana was part of the Sub Pop roster. The group's first album, *Bleach*, was released on Sub Pop in 1989.

crinosity, zemi, frictious

1. **crinosity (kree-NAHSS-uh-dee) (noun):** Hairiness. For many years, the man holding the modern world's record for longest hair was Tran Van Hay. The Vietnamese man went fifty years without a haircut, and though he never had his profuse follicles officially measured, Van Hay's hair was probably in the vicinity of twenty feet long. According to his wife, Van Hay had not washed his hair for eleven years (!) when he died, in 2010, at the age of seventy-nine.

2. **zemi (zuh-MEE) (noun):** A fetish or idol. An object that possesses a spirit and that spirit's magical potency. Zemis are especially associated with aboriginal Tainos, a tribe living in the West Indies.

3. **frictious (FRIHCK-shuss) (adj.):** Of or relating to friction, the resistance of motion of one body sliding over another. Of course, friction also occurs when people's ideas grind against one another, causing arguments.

The fake word is:
frictious

This is one of those words that just should exist, but its closest cousin is "fractious," which means "irritable and/or complaining." Fractious people create friction, of course. Take, for example, famous people who choose to whine, complain, and gripe about their "miserable" lives of facing public adoration.

Entertainment site thefrisky.com recently included an article about fractious stars who whine about not being able to get a date . . . despite being national sex symbols. The list includes *Twilight* hunk Robert Pattinson, John McCain's daughter Meghan, and crooner Kelly Clarkson. Of course, by the time you read this, these folks may no longer be available (as if you cared).

History's Most Hirsute

Tran Van Hay chose to be hairy, but some people have a rare condition called hypertrichosis that makes them excessively hairy. The condition is so rare that only fifty or so cases have been documented in history. Some conjecture that Esau, son of Isaac and Jacob's brother in the Old Testament, had hypertrichosis.

In less sensitive times, people with hypertrichosis often became sideshow stars. Julia Pastrana, born in 1834 in Mexico, was exhibited as a cross between a human and an orangutan. After her death, her corpse continued to tour the world. Russian Fedor Jeftichew became, arguably, the most famous hairy person in history. Famous promoter P.T. Barnum displayed Jeftichew as Jo-Jo the Dog-Faced Boy. Despite being fluent in three languages, Jeftichew pretended he could do little more than bark because he was raised in the wild (which, of course, he wasn't).

---

tantorosity, veldschoen, praemunire

1. **tantorosity** (TAN-tuh-rahss-uh-tee) (noun): The result of infighting among members of one's immediate family, group, organization, etc. Historically, the term often is associated with Martin Luther's break from the Roman Catholic Church, which led to the Protestant Reformation.

2. **veldschoen** (VELT-skoon) (noun): A rawhide shoe lacking nails and, typically, an insole. These South African shoes are based on aboriginal footwear spotted by Dutch settlers. Veldschoens are known as "vellies" in South African slang, and just because they sound "primitive" doesn't mean they come cheap. England's Alfred Sargent Shoes has an entire collection of "vellies" that sell for upward of two hundred pounds (more than $300).

3. **praemunire** (preem-yuh-NEAR) (noun): A legal writ, charging that one has attempted to get benefits from the Pope (excommunications, papal bulls, etc.) and use them against the king or his realm. British Parliament enacted the Statute of Praemunire during the reign of King Richard II, who, the Parliament believed, was a little too chummy (and financially beneficial) to the Pope.

The fake word is:

tantorosity

By the time Martin Luther launched his attacks on the Roman Catholic Church, he wasn't the only one who believed the Church needed some reform. But it had nothing to do with tantorosity. Some Catholic leaders took advantage of the fact that the Church *was* Christianity at that time. They made themselves rich, took numerous lovers, and, in general, lived far from saintly lives. In addition, the Church was filled with folks who sold "indulgences"—basically "get-out-of-Hell free" cards.

Luther did not believe anyone had to "buy" God's grace; it was given freely by Christ. He also argued that only the Bible—and not the Pope—was the source of divine knowledge. In addition, Luther advocated publishing the Bible in languages people actually used, instead of in Latin.

Poor Richard

Due to the deaths of his father and brother, Richard II became King of England at age ten. Perhaps due to his youth, Richard had a tendency to rely on a small group of courtiers for advice, and the advice wasn't always the best.

Most of Richard II's reign was rife with political uncertainty, and he was deposed by Henry of Bolingbroke in 1399. Bolingbroke became King Henry IV, and Richard died in captivity. Belief at the time was that Richard died of an axe wound to the head. When his tomb was later opened, no wound was found. Most likely, Richard died of starvation.

afterbath, emgalla, sprongline

1. **afterbath** (AFF-ter-bath) (noun): A solution used with photographic negatives or prints after fixation. Other odd darkroom chemicals are fixer test solutions, wetting agents, and hypo clearing agents.

2. **emgalla** (m-GALL-uh) (noun): A warthog found in southern Africa. Warthogs may not be beautiful (except to other warthogs, presumably), but they are among the hardiest of the pig family. Warthogs can live in arid areas because they can tolerate a higher-than-normal body temperature, thus conserving water they might otherwise use for cooling.

3. **sprongline** (SPRAWNG-line) (noun): A crane attachment used to lift exceptionally heavy objects. The K-10000 tower crane, by Kroll Giant Towercranes, is possibly the world's largest. The Danish company claims that the K-10000 stands 330 feet tall, has a hook radius of 269 feet, and can lift up to 132 tons.

The fake word is:
sprongline

The K-10000's first job in the United States was for General Public Utilities of Morristown, New Jersey, which intended to use it to construct the Forked River nuclear power plant. In 1979, as the crane was being assembled, the country's worst nuclear disaster struck near Harrisburg, Pennsylvania. The Three Mile Island nuclear plant was another of GPU's projects. As nuclear power plant safety expert Homer Simpson might say: "D'oh!" GPU abandoned its Forked River project, and the K-10000 was never used in its construction.

Making Photography a Snap

The French invented the earliest form of photography in the 1830s using a bitumen-covered pewter plate exposed to light. Soon after, the daguerreotype process was invented, again, in France. Daguerreotypes used silver-coated copper plates, iodine vapor, and light to create permanent images. These led to so-called wet plates, which were dunked in a solution instead of simply coated with chemicals, and these led to so-called dry plates, which could be stored and found in various sizes.

Nonetheless, photography was mostly for professionals until George Eastman's Kodak company developed roll film in the 1880s. But it wasn't until the 1940s—when 35mm film was developed—that nearly everyone started snapping photos on a regular basis. Finally, Kodak produced the first digital camera in 1991. Since then, digital photography has eclipsed print photography.

feliform, mircutal, treey

1. **feliform (FEEL-uh-form) (adj.):** Shaped like or resembling a cat. The word is not to be confused with "Feliformia," a sub-order within the order Carnivora, which includes large and small cats, hyenas, and mongooses.

2. **mircutal (muhr-CYOOT-uhl) (adj.):** Situated near the cuticles. Humans aren't the only ones with cuticles. They also can be found on plants, invertebrates, and mushrooms.

3. **treey (TREE-ee) (adj.):** Wooded or full of trees. The taiga (TIE-juh), known also as the boreal forest, makes up 27 percent of the world's forest cover. It includes most of inland Canada, as well as Alaska and some northern portions of the lower 48 states.

The fake word is:
mircutal

If you've ever wondered about the difference between mushrooms and toadstools, you're not alone. The distinction isn't entirely clear, and it's mostly a matter of etymology.

Between 1400 and 1600, the term "toadstool" referred mostly to poisonous mushrooms. Most likely, the word is derived from the German root "tod," which means "death." The stool part is related to the classic mushroom shape, which resembles a stool.

Not Too Big to Fall

One problem with really huge forests is that they are extremely tempting to logging companies. In Canada, for example, only 8 percent of the boreal forest (Canada prefers this term, while Russia prefers "taiga") is protected from development. As a result, clear-cutting of nearly vast areas has been reported in portions of the country. Most of the processed lumber winds up in the United States. Think about that the next time you wipe your butt with toilet paper, make needless photocopies, or read your local newspaper.

blad, kring, stridhana

1. **blad** (BLAD) (verb): To beat against or buffet, as wind, or to slap hard. Some publishers also use an object called a blad, which stands for Basic LAyout and Design. These mock-up booklets are used to preview a book for promotional use.

2. **kring** (KREENG) (verb): To focus on with laser-like intensity. A laser developed at the University of Michigan is believed to be the world's most intense. In a pulse lasting just one millionth-billionth of a second, Michigan's laser delivers 300 terawatts of power, three hundred times the capacity of the United States's entire electrical grid.

3. **stridhana** (STREE-duh-nuh) (noun): Property belonging to a woman, per Hindu law. Various schools of Indian law interpret stridhana differently.

The fake word is:
kring

Here are some pointers about how to attain laser-like powers of concentration when you're trying to accomplish a large task:

- Create a work space that is just for work. Don't eat, read, sleep, or do anything else there.
- Create an association between work and your desk. When you see your desk, you should think "work."
- Get rid of distractions: ringing phones, magazines, the Internet.
- Set specific—and possible—goals, and give yourself enough time to accomplish them.
- Give yourself deadlines.
- Reward success with short breaks.

The Power, the Power!

Despite much talk and some effort regarding "clean" energy, more than 50 percent of the United States's power originates in coal-burning plants. Nuclear plants account for about 20 percent of the nation's electricity, natural gas 16 percent, hydroelectric 7 percent, and oil just 2 percent.

In recent years, solar power has gained many fans. Due in part to tax breaks, U.S. homeowners have been adding solar panels to their homes in record numbers. The country is now fourth in the world in terms of energy produced by solar power. Nonetheless, the United States still lags far behind the world leader, Germany, which produces about 10,000 megawatts of solar power each year. The United States, by contrast, produces only 1,650 megawatts.

---

troofus, xat, grece

1. **troofus** (TROO-fuss) **(noun):** A small tent used especially by Australian Aborigines. Australian poet Andrew Barton "Banjo" Paterson makes frequent mention of troofuses. Paterson is best known for his poems "Waltzing Matilda" and "The Man from Snowy River."

2. **xat** (KAHT) **(noun):** A carved pole designed as a memorial to the dead by certain North American Indian tribes. Xat.com (with "xat" pronounced like "chat") is a chat-based social networking site with more than seven million users.

3. **grece** (GREECE) **(noun):** Flight of steps or one of the steps within the flight. The world's longest stairway, according to *Guinness World Records*, belongs to Spiez's Niesenbahn funicular railway. The service stairway for this Swiss attraction has 11,674 steps going up 5,476 feet, or slightly more than a mile.

The fake word is:
troofus

"Banjo" Paterson may not be a household name in the United States, but the poet, who died in 1941, is quite famous in his native country. His "Waltzing Matilda" is often referred to as the unofficial national anthem of Australia. The song refers to one who travels on foot while carrying a "matilda," or "bag," over one's shoulder. Paterson wrote the poem in 1895, and Christina Macpherson wrote a tune to accompany it in the same year.

Paterson's likeness appears on the Australian ten dollar bill, along with his poem "The Man from Snowy River." In addition, he can be found on a postage stamp, and Gold Coast's A. B. Paterson College is named for the poet, whose nickname derived from a pseudonym adopted by the young Paterson.

One Step at a Time

Every year, the steps of the Niesenbahn funicular railway are host to a grueling competition. The winner in 2010, Tobias Walser, reached the 11,674th step in 1:02:38. Competitive stair-climbing has become a major sport, and those who compete suggest marathons are for wimps. Perhaps they're right.

The Niesenbahn competition is itself wimpy when compared to Germany's Saxonian Mt. Everest Marathon. Runners must run up and down 397 stairs one hundred times . . . or a distance equivalent to attaining the summit of Mt. Everest twice. Only one woman and eleven men managed to complete the Mt. Everest Marathon in 2001, the first year of the competition. The event's record holders are Kurt Hess, who completed the punishing pursuit in 14:48:28 in 2007, and Ulrike Baars, who finished in 17:43:29 in 2008.

---

placidamente, irreal, talp

1. **placidamente (plah-chee-duh-MENT-ee) (adv. or adj.):** In music, to play placidly or calmly. A musical synonym is calmando. Some placidamente opposites are crescendo, fortissimo, and marcato.

2. **irreal: (EAR-eel) (adj.)** Of or related to something not real. Famous people who have believed in UFOs might surprise you. Included on the list are former President Jimmy Carter, Gen. Douglas MacArthur, and FBI founder J. Edgar Hoover.

3. **talp (TALP) (noun):** A body of water that is dying due to extreme weather, a natural disaster, or human interference.

The fake word is:

talp

If talp *were* a word, then a perfect example of one would be the former Soviet Union's Aral Sea, which once was one of the four largest lakes in the entire world. In 1960, the Aral covered 26,300 square miles. That year, however, its major tributaries were diverted for irrigation projects, and the Aral Sea has been shrinking ever since. It is now ten percent of its original size and has dried up into four separate lakes.

These eerie bodies of water were once brimming with fish, but they're now all but dead. Once part of a major seaway, the lakes now reveal rusting wrecked ships jutting out of what once was the bottom of the sea. Even worse, fertilizers, chemicals, and other poisonous items dumped into the lake have mixed with the soil of the former sea bottom. Winds carry the eroded and toxic soil all over the region.

Take Us to Your Leader!

The most famous "UFO crash" took place in 1947 near Roswell, New Mexico. In the summer of that year, local Army officials put out a press release that said soldiers had recovered a "flying disc" from a ranch. The media jumped on the story, and soon after the Army published a retraction, changing the otherwordly sounding "disk" to the more quotidian "radar-tracking balloon." The story went cold and was forgotten until in an interest in UFOs landed in popular culture in the late 1970s.

Since then, people have come out of the ether to argue that the balloon really *was* some sort of disk, and not just a run-of-the-mill disk—it was a flying saucer.

---

teponaxtle, worpful, samogon

1. **teponaxtle** (tuh-puh-NAHST-lee) (noun): An Aztec-derived Mexican drum. Drums have been around for thousands of years. Based on excavations, ancient Mesopotamians were rocking out more than 3,000 years ago.

2. **worpful** (WARP-full) (adj.): Of or related to prehistoric inventions. Yale University scientist Barbee Ellendow's *The Cycles of Worpful Societies* was a cause célèbre in the late 1950s.

3. **samogon** (SAHM-o-GOHN) (noun): Homemade brew, especially homemade vodka. Russia's first "legal moonshine," Kosogorov Samogon, first reached the market in 2003. It costs about $30 to $40 per liter; "legal" vodka costs closer to $10 per liter.

The fake word is:
worpful

Stone Age people didn't have rocks in their heads, and they proved that necessity is the mother of invention. Tribes from throughout the world developed similar inventions that we modern folks use today.

Og and his buddies came up with the needle and thread some 15,000 years ago because they needed to make their warm furs and skins fit to their bodies. Early needles were made from bones, and thread was made of tendons or leather. How did they get those skins? With their bows and arrows, of course. These handy devices were invented at roughly the same time.

Unfortunately, Stone Age lords and ladies had to subsist on raw, or possibly dried, food for thousands of years because, most likely, fire wasn't "invented" until about 10,000 years ago.

Gin in the Bathtub?

It depends on whom you ask. "Bathtub gin" was America's favorite, reasonably easy way to get loaded during Prohibition. Flappers and philosophers alike drank this rotgut stuff by the gallon. It was made of cheap grain alcohol to which drinkers would add flavorings such as juniper berry juice.

Some contend the beverage got its name because it actually was mixed in bathtubs and allowed to "steep" in the tub until it was slightly more palatable than, say, lighter fluid. Others, however, say the hooch was not mixed in tubs at all. The large bottles most commonly used for making gin were too tall to be topped off with water from the sink, so they were put under the bathtub taps instead.

---

nalophile, acrophony, dreddour

1. **nalophile (NAIL-uh-file) (noun):** One who studies, or is simply intrigued by dry creekbeds, dry gullies, dry lakes, etc.

2. **acrophony (uh-KRAHF-uh-nee) (noun):** An alphabet term referring to the naming of a letter by a word with a beginning sound the same as that which the letter represents. Greek letter names are acrophonic, for example: alpha, beta, delta, etc.

3. **dreddour (DREAD-uhr) (noun):** A combination of the words "dread" and "terror" denoting something that causes this mixture in someone. Fear of public speaking continues to top many lists of items that raise dreddour in the average person.

The fake word is:
nalophile

Perhaps the world's most famous dry lake—at least for Ufologists, or those who study UFOs—is Nevada's Groom Lake, the site of so-called Area 51.

Groom Lake was used for bombing and artillery practice during World War II, but it began to gain its air of surreptitiousness in 1955, when Lockheed Corporation used Groom Lake to test its super-secret U-2 spy plane. To this day, the government uses Area 51 to test prototype aircraft.

As a result, many have come to believe that Area 51 is more than just a place to distribute defense spending. It is nothing less than a veritable zoo for extraterrestrials and their captured aircraft.

Odd Fears

Who isn't afraid of heights at least some of the time? Is there anyone who can't at the very least sympathize with those who fear confined spaces or violent crime or death? Some people, however, feel "dreddour" about the most bizarre things:

- **ablutophobia:** fear of bathing or cleaning
- **anthophobia:** fear of flowers
- **chorophobia:** fear of dancing
- **coulrophobia:** fear of clowns
- **oikophobia:** fear of household appliances
- **paraskevidekatriaphobia:** fear of Friday the 13th
- **phobophobia:** fear of having a phobia

---

morepork, Zaparan, listern

1. **morepork (MORE-pork) (noun):** A term used chiefly in Australia to signify a dull-witted person.

2. **Zaparan (ZAHP-uhr-uhn) (adj., usually capitalized):** Of or relating to the Zaparo, a tribe living in the Peruvian borderlands, or the tribe's language. Zaparan is very close to going the way of Latin. Only 150 to 170 ethnic Zaparans exist today, and very few of them have any knowledge of the tribe's once-healthy language.

3. **listern (LIST-urn) (noun):** A small dish designed to hold family keepsakes. Listerns with exquisite designs were all the rage in Victorian England, and well-preserved examples can sell for hundreds, even thousands of dollars, on eBay.

The fake word is:

listern

Why would you need a nonexistent listern when you could just take up scrapbooking? As early as the fifteenth century and the advent of affordable paper, people began to compile poems, recipes, letters, you name it, in so-called commonplace books. As photography became available to everyone, scrapbooks also became hybrids with photo albums.

Then along came Utah's Marielen Christensen, widely regarded as the person who transformed scrapbooking from a family affair into a huge industry. In the early 1980s, Christensen published *Keeping Memories Alive* and opened a still-extant scrapbooking store. Her twist on an old-fashioned idea took off, and now craft supply stores should feature shrines to Christensen, who keeps them alive well into the digital age.

The Deadly Qualities of Rubber

In prehistoric times, the Zaparo were one of the largest and most powerful tribes in the Amazonian region. More than 100,000 spoke Zaparan. Like many other native peoples, European settlers decimated Zaparan people and culture upon their arrival, giving "gifts" of disease and enslavement. Nonetheless, the Zaparo managed to survive in fairly healthy numbers up to the twentieth century.

As automobiles became a necessity for most Westerners, a new group of "settlers" arrived, eager to plunder rubber trees for making tires. The Zaparo were used as cheap—let's just call it slave—labor, which disrupted Zaparan communities. As Zaparans found themselves farther and farther from home, they married with members of other tribes and adopted one of the Quechua languages, which are still used by as many as eight million indigenous people of the Americas.

---

quadrel, screemish, flaucht

1. **quadrel (KWAHD-ruhl) (noun):** A square building block, not confined to any one type of material. Quadrel also was a video game, released in 1991, in which players created blocks using one of four possible colors.

2. **screemish (SCREEM-ish) (adj.):** Something squishy or indeterminate. The word could refer to a pile of dough or unshaped clay, or it could refer to one's plans.

3. **flaucht (FLAKT) (noun):** A flash of fire or lightning. The Democratic Republic of Congo gets the most lightning strikes in the world, in part due to its location near the equator, which is "summery" year-round. Annually, each square kilometer of Congo receives more than 150 lightning strikes.

The fake word is:

screemish

One man who made hard cash out of something squishy is Arthur "Art" Clokey. Clokey was a stop-motion animation pioneer, whose commercials for Coca-Cola and Budweiser are classics of early television. But Clokey's real love was clay, and he made the most of it starting in 1955.

That year, Clokey created a short film that starred a nondescript-shaped, anthropomorphic piece of clay who, thanks to the miracle of stop-motion, took on a personality and got into adventures. From the film *Gumbasia* (a pun on Walt Disney's *Fantasia*) came the still-beloved characters Gumby and Pokey.

In the early 1960s, Clokey began his other contribution to popular culture, *Davey and Goliath*. This stop-motion, clay-figure-peopled series was sponsored by the Lutheran Church and was used to introduce children to Christian values. "Davey" was Davey Hansen, and "Goliath" was his talking dog.

Lightning Strikes Me Again

U.S. Park Ranger Roy Sullivan still holds a record no one is looking to beat: the most lightning strikes survived by a single person. The first time Sullivan was struck was in 1942, when he went inside a fire lookout tower to avoid a thunderstorm. He wound up being struck six more times over the next thirty-five years. Finally, six years after the seventh strike, which took place in 1977, Sullivan took matters into his own hands. Lightning couldn't kill him, but unrequited love could. Allegedly, spurned advances were the reason Sullivan died in 1983 from a self-inflicted gunshot wound.

fromacious, minacious, oblivionize

1. **fromacious** (froh-MAY-shuss) (adj.): Relating to carcinogens that attack the extremities. Fromacious germs can be airborne or passed through human contact.

2. **minacious** (muh-NAY-shuss) (adj.): Of or related to a menacing, threatening character. History and literature are filled with minacious characters because, let's face it, everybody loves to hate bad guys.

3. **oblivionize** (oh-BLIV-ee-uh-nize) (verb): To consign to oblivion. God did this when he gave up on Sodom and Gomorrah and when everyone except Noah and his family just didn't seem worth keeping on Earth any longer.

The fake word is:

fromacious

The world is full of carcinogens, sometimes making one wonder if there is anything that *doesn't* cause cancer. Well, you are in luck! According to canceravoid.com, a website from India, there are at least five common things on this planet that will not send you to chemotherapy.

- Deodorant
- Power lines
- Bras
- Breast implants
- Stress

Of course, the site doesn't seem to be much of authority, so you might, you know, actually want to talk to your doctor.

Villains and Economics

The etymology of "villain" is proof that history has always been on the side of the winners.

The word comes from the Latin word *villanus*, which means simply "farmhand." Farmhands are not, of course, inherently evil. So, how did this harmless word come to denote black-hatted bad guys forcing peacemaking sheriffs into showdowns at High Noon?

Those who worked in the soil, menial workers of their day, were not going to be found among the upper classes. As a result, *villanus* and its derivatives began to refer to people who were not chivalrous. If you're not chivalrous, then you'll commit all manner of horrible crimes. Over time, a word that once referred merely to someone poor began to refer to someone evil . . . or at least generically bad.

---

fugleman, Hercynian, fabophile

1. **fugleman (FOO-gull-man) (noun):** One who leads a group, especially a trained soldier who serves at the head of a drill line as a model for exercises. The word derives from a German word meaning "wing," so a fugleman is also a "wingman."

2. **Hercynian (her-SIN-ee-uhn) (adj., usually capitalized):** Describes the Earth-folding and mountain building in the Eastern hemisphere during the Paleozoic period. The Paleozoic Era lasted from 543 million to 248 million years ago.

3. **fabophile (FAB-uh-file) (noun):** One who studies The Beatles, known as the "Fab Four." The term began to pop up on Beatles-related websites around the turn of the present century.

The fake word is:
fabophile

During The Beatles's short run as an active group, many people were considered (or considered themselves) "the fifth Beatle." Perhaps the most famous was New York disc jockey "Murray the K" (Murray Kaufman), who was among the first to play the group's records in America.

Kaufman wasn't just one of the Fab Four's first fans. He also helped Bob Dylan transition from his folk period to his rock period. When Kaufman introduced Dylan to a hostile rock-shunning crowd at Forest Hills in 1965, he told the angry fans, "It's not rock, it's not folk, it's a new thing called Dylan."

Giving You Wings

After Paul McCartney left The Beatles, he became the world's most famous "wingman" when he formed his group called Wings. The lineup of the band shifted constantly during its existence, which lasted from 1971 to 1981. At its core were McCartney himself; McCartney's wife, Linda; and Denny Laine, a former member of The Moody Blues.

Although no one would argue that Wings was as important culturally as McCartney's first band, the group had a steady stream of hits throughout the 1970s. Wings earned six number-one records in the United States, including "My Love," "Band on the Run," and "Listen to What the Man Said." Soon after songwriting partner John Lennon's death, McCartney suspended work on a Wings record, and the group, which as noted was never a solid unit of people, disintegrated.

---

blatherskite, flambit, juck

1. **blatherskite (BLATH-uhr-skite) (noun):** Nonsense and blather, or one who is given to being blustery, long-winded, and, typically, incompetent. According to teenagers, all parents are blatherskites.

2. **flambit (FLAM-bit) (noun):** A quick move in chess, designed to confuse opponents. Whether or not he used flambits, chess master Garry Kasparov proved in 1996 that man is mightier than machine when he beat chess computer Deep Blue.

3. **juck (JUHCK) (verb):** To make the noise of a partridge that is settling down for a night's rest. According to legend, the first partridge appeared when Daedalus, a mythological Greek genius who found his way out of a minotaur's labyrinth, threw his nephew off a roof in a fit of jealous rage.

The fake word is:
flambit

Garry Kasparov won the first match against Deep Blue, but in 1997 the computer had the last (virtual) laugh.

In May of 1997, the IBM-developed chess computer won a six-game match against Kasparov. The Russian chess master quickly cried foul (or its Russian equivalent), but the folks at IBM thumbed their collective noses and dismantled Deep Blue soon after. No flambit involved here.

Come On, Get Happy!

For four years at the dawn of the 1970s, America's most famous family was a group of musicians who traveled in a brightly colored bus and sang pop hits most people either loved or loathed.

The Partridge Family was an ABC television show loosely based on The Cowsills, a family of musicians who had hits with bubblegum pop confections like "The Rain, the Park, and Other Things." Although the musical sitcom was built around Oscar-winning actress Shirley Jones, her real-life stepson, David Cassidy, quickly became the main focus of the show . . . at least to giggly tweens of that era who thought "Keith Partridge" was totally dreamy.

The Partridge Family became so popular that life soon began to imitate art, and the "group," most of whom were not actual musicians, began to tour and record albums. The group's best-known song is "I Think I Love You," sung by Cassidy (who *could* actually sing, just like his stepmother), written by Tony Romeo. The tune hit number one in 1970.

---

fubsy, auwai, trungish

1. **fubsy (FUHB-zee) (adj.):** Chubby, squat, as an individual. This chiefly British word might best be exemplified by fubsy, chiefly British comedian Benny Hill.

2. **auwai (OO-wee) (noun):** Hawaiian term denoting an irrigation channel. The Auwai of Nuuanu Valley is one of Hawaii's most endangered sites due to its transition from agricultural to residential use. At one time, these auwai were maintained by a state agency, but now they are mostly controlled by individual property owners who don't always have other people's needs in mind.

3. **trungish (TRUN-gish) (adj.):** Of or related to one who avoids crowds, especially one who avoids them due to fear of making small talk.

The fake word is:
trungish

Making small talk can be daunting, but it can also be rewarding. If you can make a connection with a stranger then, who knows, somewhere down the road that stranger may hire you as a VP at her widget-making business. Consider these tips the next time you find yourself forced to make small talk:

- Pre-plan. Come up with three conversational gambits before you enter the party, business meeting, etc.
- Say "hello" first and leave the onus for conversation on the other person.
- Listen more than you talk. People will consider you brilliant, and you won't even have to open your mouth very often!
- Gain at least a reasonable grasp of current events, and save trivia/reflections about them for gambits should a conversation lag.

Big-Boned Comics

Even during Shakespeare's day, actors offering comic relief often were pleasingly plump. The connection between fubsiness and humor has continued throughout entertainment history.

Roscoe "Fatty" Arbuckle became one of the first rotund comedians to gain enormous fame on the silver screen. He was, perhaps, Hollywood's biggest star (no pun intended) during the 1910s, possessing a contract worth $1 million a year (the equivalent of $23 million today).

Arbuckle left audiences rolling in the aisles until he was accused of raping bit-player Virginia Rappe, who died soon after the incident. After multiple trials, Arbuckle was exonerated, but his career was never the same again. He descended into alcoholism and died in 1933 at the age of forty-six.

---

klaut, Clausewitz, elaphine

1. **klaut (CLOT) (noun):** Early work by an established author that, while not very polished, is not considered juvenilia. Some authors, such as Thomas Mann, skip this stage altogether and begin their careers with novels that become classics. Mann's first novel was *Buddenbrooks*, a thinly veiled history of his family.

2. **Clausewitz (CLAWS-vitz) (noun, usually capitalized):** A military strategy expert. Carl von Clausewitz, who died in 1831, was a Prussian army officer and expert on military science.

3. **elaphine (ELL-uh-feen) (adj.):** Of, relating to, or resembling the red deer. The red deer is one of the world's largest deer species, with populations in Europe, western Asia, and central Asia.

The fake word is:
klaut

After two novels that bear little resemblance to his later masterworks, William Faulkner composed his klaut (or would have, if the word existed). Published originally as *Sartoris* and later, in a "director's cut" as *Flags in the Dust*, Faulkner's third novel is a transition from juvenilia to maturity. The story traces the demise of the once-powerful Sartoris family, in much the same way that *Buddenbrooks* traces the demise of the once-powerful Buddenbrooks family.

While it does not achieve the groundbreaking stature of his next work, *The Sound and the Fury*, *Sartoris* is an important work in Faulkner's canon because it makes use of one of the author's consistent themes: the death of Southern aristrocracy. It introduces Yoknapatawpha County, the mythical region that is the scene of Faulkner's greatest works; and it introduces Byron Snopes, the first of the viral, no-account Snopes clan, which is largely responsible (as far as Faulkner is concerned) for the demise of the great Southern families.

The Fog of War

Clausewitz's most lasting contribution to popular culture may be his concept of "the fog of war." In essence, the concept refers to the inability of political and military leaders to gain enough intelligence to make the best decisions in the midst of war. Unfortunately, by making poor decisions, soldiers, sailors, marines, and airmen die.

plainstanes, gwapple, smaik

1. **plainstanes (PLANE-stanes) (noun):** A sidewalk made of flagstones, common in Scotland. Americans tend to call pedestrian paths beside roadways "sidewalks," while Brits tend to call these same paths "pavement."

2. **gwapple (GWOHP-uhl) (verb):** To beg for mercy. The word originates in Algonquin Indian dialect, and is referenced in early "captivity narratives"—works written by English settlers who were taken prisoner by Native Americans.

3. **smaik (SMAKE) (noun):** A scoundrel or rascal; a rogue. These are the gentlemen we love to hate. They're not necessarily evil . . . just self-serving—albeit dashing.

The fake word is:

gwapple

The most famous captivity narrative is that of Mary Rowlandson. Rowlandson's *The Sovereignty and Goodness of God: Being a Narrative of the Captivity and Restoration of Mrs. Mary Rowlandson*, was the *Harry Potter* of its day in terms of popularity.

England-born Mary White's family moved to Massachusetts in 1650 when White was just thirteen. White married minister Thomas Rowlandson in 1656, and the couple had three surviving children. Mary Rowlandson and her children were among captives taken by local Indian tribes in 1675. She remained in captivity for about four months before being ransomed.

Rowlandson's book not only was popular in its day, but it continues to be read because it gives modern-day readers a glimpse into the Puritan mind. Note, for example, the title of her work. Despite being enslaved and watching her youngest daughter die during their captivity, Rowlandson never failed to believe in the "goodness of God."

Aaarrrggghh!

Edward Teach, Blackbeard, who gained his nickname due to his hirsute chin and frightening appearance, was the scourge of the West Indies and the American colonies during the early eighteenth century. Blackbeard's biggest "success" was his blockade of the port of Charleston, South Carolina, which netted Teach and his compatriots a bevy of blackguard booty. Allegedly, he buried much of this treasure somewhere in North Carolina's Outer Banks, and it remains there to this day, guarded by the fearsome ghost of its plunderer.

Blackbeard died in 1718, during a battle with members of an ad hoc Virginia militia.

---

pfleiderer, vetturino, drantalgate

1. **pfleiderer** (FLY-duhr-uhr) (noun): In rayon manufacturing, a machine used to shred cellulose sheets into tiny bits. In addition to its use in clothing, rayon also serves as the filling in Zippo lighters.

2. **vetturino** (ved-uh-REE-no) (noun): One who drives a vettura, an Italian carriage often driven for hire. Ferrari's recently developed hybrid vehicle is called the HY-KERS vettura laboratorio.

3. **drantalgate** (DRANT-uhl-gut) (adj.): Of or resembling a pig's snout. Pigs, like humans, can get sunburns. That's why they cover themselves in mud; it acts as sunblock.

The fake word is:
drantalgate

Pigs have lent themselves to numerous sayings, including the concept of "putting lipstick on a pig," which suggests that however you dress up something unpleasant, it's still unpleasant.

During the 2008 election, then-candidate Barack Obama got into some pig-appropriate mudslinging, referring to some of Sarah Palin's policies. Palin, at the time, was the running mate of John McCain, who was competing with Obama for the presidency.

The tempest in a teapot led Republicans to demand an apology, and many who opposed Obama inferred that Obama wasn't referring to policies; he was, instead, making a comment about Palin's appearance. For a few days, Obama was accused high and low of being sexist. He dismissed the whole situation as silly, and shortly thereafter the imbroglio passed.

The Hall of Zippos

How many lighters can claim their own museum? Not many, but Zippo can. The American-made lighter company, which offers a complete lifetime warranty for its products, has a 15,000-square-foot museum devoted to its two chief product lines: Zippo lighters and Case knives.

The entrance to the Bradford, Pennsylvania, museum features fourteen streetlights shaped like giant Zippos. Dwarfing these is a forty-foot lighter with a pulsating flame atop a massive three-bladed Case pocketknife. The museum is, of course, filled with examples of Zippos and Case knives. (Hey, kids! Forget Disneyland! Let's go look at some lighters!)

---

kabler, flanconnade, pallone

1. **kabler (KAY-blur) (verb):** To move in a way resembling the motion of a small child. Scottish poet Robert Burns, of "Auld Lang Syne" fame, used this word extensively in his works.

2. **flanconnade (FLAN-kuh-nade) (noun):** A fencing move that ends in a thrust under an opponent's arm. The art of fencing began during the Italian Renaissance, but it was perfected in the eighteenth century by the French.

3. **pallone (puh-LONE) (noun):** An Italian game resembling tennis, played by striking a leather ball with a cylindrical guard worn over one's hand and wrist. The word is Italian for an inflated ball; etymologically, it is similar to "balloon."

The fake word is:
kabler

The poem, "Auld Lang Syne," which translates roughly to "long, long ago," is a staple of New Year's Eve parties. Drunk, weepy folks say goodbye to the past year by (badly) singing the poem ascribed to Robert Burns.

Burns didn't in fact write "Auld Lang Syne." You might say he perfected it. In addition to writing original verse, Scotland's Burns also collected national folk songs, and the New Year's Eve staple has been around since at least the sixteenth century. The tune to which the words are sung also belong to the Scottish folk tradition.

So I Made a Crumby Mistake

One of literature's greatest anti-heroes, J. D. Salinger's Holden Caulfield, has a "fencing accident" at the start of *The Catcher in the Rye*, and it acts as a catalyst to his nervous breakdown. Caulfield is manager of his prep school's fencing team, but he leaves the foils (blades) and other equipment on the subway, causing his team to forfeit a match.

Possibly, Caulfield is just being passive-aggressive, angry that he's only "the goddam manager" and not a competitor. Or, perhaps Caulfield's negligence demonstrates that he is already starting to crack up. Either way, Caulfield's teammates become justifiably upset, and soon after, Caulfield leaves Pencey Prep and disappears for a few aimless days in New York City.

spilter, tink, unguligrade

1. **spilter (SPILL-tuhr) (verb):** To break or damage by throwing a rock or stone. The word suggests that the action was done specifically to cause damage.

2. **tink (TEENK) (verb):** To emit a tinkling sound, as a small bell. "Tink" also is the nickname of perennially popular fairy Tinker Bell . . . or, as she is sometimes known, Tinkerbell.

3. **unguligrade (UHN-gyuhl-uh-grade) (adj.):** Walking on hooves. Hoofed animals come in one of two orders. If they have an even number of toes, they belong to Artiodactyla. If they have an odd number of toes, they belong to Perissodactyla.

The fake word is:
spilter

The act of stoning someone to death is familiar to many Westerners because of its appearance in the Bible. Unfortunately, the act is still practiced today. The "benefit" of stoning is that the "stoners" don't have to feel personally responsible for the death of the "stonee." Who knows who threw the rock that actually killed the condemned? As of 2010, Afghanistan, Saudi Arabia, Somalia, Sudan, Nigeria, and Iran still use stoning as a method of execution.

In literature, one of the most famous uses of stoning occurs in Shirley Jackson's "The Lottery." Jackson's story takes place in a small town that has a special "lottery" every year to ensure a good harvest. The lottery consists of stoning to death the "winner" of eponymous lottery. Some believe Jackson's story is a commentary on what she considered the small-mindedness of her Vermont hometown.

I Won't Grow Up

Tinkerbell is best known as a popular Walt Disney fairy who covers the walls, bedspreads, backpacks, etc., of young girls around the world. In effect, she is Peter Pan's sidekick, even though her creator, J. M. Barrie, considered her only "a common fairy."

Peter Pan, a boy who loathes growing up and who has magical adventures, was first introduced by Barrie in *The Little White Bird* (1902). The section of Barrie's novel containing the story of Peter Pan became so popular that it was reprinted as a separate book, *Peter Pan in Kensington Gardens*. Subsequently, Barrie wrote a play—*Peter Pan, or The Boy Who Wouldn't Grow Up*—featuring Peter Pan, which became a huge hit.

criticaster, raffize, whillaballoo

4. **criticaster (CRIT-uh-cass-tuhr) (noun):** A critic who is inferior or even contemptible. Far from an inferior critic, H. L. Mencken is credited with helping spur the so-called Southern Renaissance after he wrote about the dearth of art below the Mason-Dixon Line in his essay "The Sahara of the Bozart."

5. **raffize (rah-FEEZ) (verb):** To bleach fabric for decorative purposes. The most famous "branch" of raffizing is the tie-dyed T-shirt, popularized in the 1960s.

6. **whillaballoo (WILL-uh-buh-loo) (noun):** Chiefly Scotch and Irish variant of "hullabaloo." *Hullabaloo* was the name of a brief rival of Dick Clark's *American Bandstand*.

The fake word is:

raffize

Tie-dyed T-shirts may call to mind Woodstock, VW vans, and granny glasses, but tie-dying (not raffizing) itself pre-dates the 1960s by more than a thousand years.

Pre-Columbian Peruvians were making tie-dyed cloth as early as 500 to 800 A.D. Japanese were perfecting the art of shibori, or tie-dyeing, at about the same time. In addition, various African countries also developed methods of tie-dyeing fabric.

As far as the 1960s are concerned, hippies and neo-hippies alike have unsung hero Ann Thomas to thank. Known as "Tie-Dye Annie," Thomas "dropped out" of her day job at Capitol Records to work in the Free Store, a hippie favorite in San Francisco's Haight-Ashbury district. Thomas's designs became popular with local bands, and those bands helped disseminate her designs—and the concept of tie-dying in general—to the masses.

What's All the Hubbub, Bub?

The television variety series *Hullabaloo* lasted only one season, from 1965 to 1966. Perhaps it wasn't entirely successful because it wasn't quite hip enough. Each week's episode was hosted by a different performer, and most of these performers did not have names that strike us as being synonymous with hip today: Paul Anka, Frankie Avalon, Petula Clark. *Hullabaloo* was replaced by the popular and somewhat-more-hip *The Monkees*, a show featuring a Beatles-like group.

---

scrantish, graphospasm, yirr

1. **scrantish (SCRAN-tish) (adj.):** Bulky and difficult to lift, as a load. A sofa, for example, is probably the most scrantish of all loads.

2. **graphospasm (GRAFF-uh-spazz-uhm) (noun):** The International Scientific Vocabulary term for common writer's cramp. Since science is an ever-spurting fountain of neologisms, the ISV is used to keep track of them in order to benefit scientists around the world.

3. **yirr (YIHR) (verb):** To growl or snarl like a dog. There are between 500 and 600 dog breeds in the world.

The fake word is:

scrantish

If scrantish puts you in mind of Scranton, Pennsylvania, then that's because it was the "inspiration" for the word. Although best known as the home of the nonexistent Dunder Mifflin paper company (featured on *The Office*), Scranton actually was one of the nation's chief producers of phonograph records during the years that records were the world's chief method of enjoying recorded music.

The Scranton Button Company, founded in 1865, began to produce phonograph records in the 1920s. During the height of production, the company made the "platters that matter" for companies ranging from Emerson to Brunswick to Vocalion. In 1946, the Scranton Button Company was bought by Capitol Records, which used the plant to make records up to the end of the vinyl era.

A Dog-Eat-Dog World

Dogs all descend from domesticated versions of the gray wolf, which first became man's best friend some 15,000 years ago. Then, as now, dogs were useful for hunting, protection, and companionship. Some East Asian countries also consider them quite tasty.

The practice of raising dogs for human consumption dates back thousands of years in countries such as Korea, China, and Vietnam. The most popular Korean, um, dog dish is gaejang-guk, which is basically chili with dog meat. While many Westerners consider the consumption of dogs horrific, that doesn't stop the United States from euthanizing between three to four million dogs in animal shelters each year.

pule, Kraepelinian, zaph

1. **pule (PYOOL) (verb):** To make a sad moaning sound; to whine or to whimper. Fortunately, in "The Hollow Men," T. S. Eliot decided to say the world will end with a "whimper" and not with a "pule." It just doesn't sound as good, does it?

2. **Kraepelinian (KREPP-uh-lin-ee-uhn) (adj., usually capitalized):** Of or relating Emil Kraepelin and/or his psychiatric classification system. Kraepelin was among the first to posit that psychiatric diseases often result from biological and genetic sources.

3. **zaph (ZAFF) (noun):** A computer language that flourished briefly in the late 1980s. The first programming languages actually predate the invention of the computer.

The fake word is:
zaph

Jacquard looms were among the first inventions to use programming languages.

Joseph Marie Jacquard invented his mechanized loom in 1801. This early form of mechanized mass production was controlled by punched cards, which fed designs to the looms.

The looms merely followed the design of the cards and did not do any actual "computing" with them, but Jacquard's invention is considered a milestone in both computers and programming languages.

A Poet by Any Other Name

Thomas Stearns Eliot was an American by birth and a Brit by choice. Before his death in 1965, Eliot became the poet many consider the greatest of the twentieth century. Before writing "The Hollow Men," a poem denigrating what Eliot considered the shortcomings of the Treaty of Versailles, which ended World War I, Eliot made his name and reputation with "The Love Song of J. Alfred Prufrock." Eliot used stream of consciousness techniques to elevate a navel-gazing, love-lacking loser to the height of a literary god.

Stream of consciousness, which gives readers a glimpse into the churning minds of fictional characters, is one of literary modernism's most important legacies. Eliot wasn't the only modernist to use it, of course. Others included James Joyce, especially in the "Penelope" section of *Ulysses*, and William Faulkner, especially in *The Sound and the Fury* and *As I Lay Dying*.

---

stramlished, angild, somedeal

1. **stramlished (STRAM-lished) (adj.):** Beaten or damaged by heavy winds. To this day, the worst natural disaster in American history was a hurricane that hit Galveston, Texas, in 1900. The Category Four hurricane (sustained winds of 131 to 155 miles per hour) killed 6,000 people.

2. **angild (AHN-gild) (noun):** An Anglo-Saxon era form of compensation made as one payment at a fixed value for an injury made to a person or his/her property. The Germanic Anglo-Saxons took control of Great Britain in the fifth century A.D. and ruled until the Norman conquest of 1066.

3. **somedeal (SUHM-DEAL) (adv.):** To some degree, to a certain extent; somewhat. Perhaps this should replace the painfully overused "whatever."

The fake word is:
stramlished

Hurricanes have wreaked havoc since long before recorded history, but here are some of modern times' worst:

- The Okeechobee Hurricane of 1928 killed 2,500 people and caused the equivalent of $300 million worth of damage in Florida, the Bahamas and Puerto Rico.
- In 1992, Hurricane Andrew caused $30 billion in damages to south Florida.
- The bizarre movement of 1994's Hurricane Gordon—which went from Central America to Florida to North Carolina and then back to Florida—killed 1,145 people.
- Hurricane Katrina not only devastated portions of New Orleans and the Gulf Coast in 2005, but it also killed nearly 2,000 people and became a politically charged storm. Some felt that the government's response to the disaster was much too slow and led directly to some of the storm's deaths.

Whatever

The so-called Valley Girls, pampered young ladies living in California's San Fernando Valley, first started using this word religiously in the 1980s. In effect, it means, "What you're saying is irrelevant, so shut up," or something equally rude and dismissive. At the turn of the present century, "whatever" began to pop up in the mouths of teenagers (and adults, for that matter). Marist College polls in both 2009 and 2010 rated "whatever" the most annoying phrase in a conversation.

eenamost, barant, illuminism

1. **eenamost** (EE-nuh-most) (adv.): A contraction of even and almost equivalent to the word "nearly." This is a classic example of what author Lewis Carroll called a "portmanteau word." A portmanteau is a suitcase, and the idea is that if you were to throw a couple of words in a suitcase and hurl them around, new words would be the result.

2. **barant** (buh-RANT) (noun): A reclining wingback chair. The first recliners were made in Michigan in the 1920s.

3. **illuminism** (ih-LOOM-uh-nizz-uhm) (noun): Belief in or claim to possess superiority of a personal, intellectual, cultural, or spiritual manner, not accessible to humankind in general. The word shares the same root as "Illuminati," the supposed "shadowy figures" behind most world powers.

The fake word is:

barant

Monroe, Michigan, cousins Edward Knabusch and Edwin Shoemaker helped to make the world a lazier place by inventing the first recliner, incidentally not ever called a barant. The two quit their day jobs in 1927 in order to build the American dream. They started with shoes before moving on to furniture. In 1928, they designed a wooden model recliner. In 1929, they began making upholstered models and settled on the name "La-Z-Boy."

Just as they got their business off the ground, the stock market crashed. When customers couldn't buy chairs with money, the cousins took livestock or other items for trade. The La-Z-Boy has been a success ever since.

Twas Brillig!

Arguably, Lewis Carroll's most famous poem is "Jabberwocky," which is chock-full of portmanteau words. It first appeared in *Through the Looking-Glass, and What Alice Found There*. Although somewhat puzzling, "Jabberwocky" remains a classic because its plot is easy to follow, despite neologisms embedded within the poem like nuts in a brownie. In "Jabberwocky," a young man goes out to fight a beast called a Jabberwock, is successful, and returns home to much acclaim.

Along the way, readers are confronted with words like "slithy," which appears to be a conflation of the words "slimy" and "slithery," and "frumious," which uses pieces of the words "furious" and "frightening." In addition, Carroll made up some words that do not appear to be related to other words. Some of them, such as "chortle," have become a permanent part of our lexicon.

behindhand, urceiform, elatory

1. **behindhand (bee-HIND-hand) (adv. or adj.):** To be in debt; to be behind the times; tardy. As of spring 2011, America's national debt had climbed at a rate of about $4.07 billion a day since September of 2007!

2. **urceiform (UHRSS-uh-form) (adj.):** Shaped like an ancient Roman pitcher with one handle. Most Roman pitchers were made of terra cotta, a clay-based, unglazed ceramic.

3. **elatory (EE-luh-tore-ee) (adj.):** Characterized by sudden bursts of excitement. Children, as parents and teachers know, are quite susceptible to elatory actions.

The fake word is:
elatory

One reason so many children are "elatory" is ADHD. Since the 1970s, Attention Deficit Hyperactivity Disorder has become a catch-all for all manner of children's poor behavior: acting out, not paying attention, not staying on task, being unfocused, etc. We used to scold these children and try to force them to behave. Now, we medicate them.

Even though children are most often associated with ADHD, more than half of diagnosed children continue to show signs of the neurological disorder into adulthood.

Hand Me That Pitcher, Molly!

Molly Pitcher is a name that many children still learn when being introduced to the American Revolution. Most likely, she was a composite of many patriotic women, especially two particular women.

Mary Ludwig Hayes (nicknamed Molly) followed her husband into battle, which was a not uncommon practice. These so-called camp followers would cook and clean for their husbands. Sometimes they would even get involved in battles. Revolutionary-era cannons needed a steady supply of water, and soldiers would call out to Mary (and probably others), "Molly! Pitcher!" One day, as history or legend suggests, Hayes actually took over firing the cannon after her husband was wounded.

Margaret Corbin is another possible source for "Molly Pitcher." Her story is very similar to Hayes's. When her husband John was wounded, Corbin took his place at a cannon during the defense of Fort Washington.

---

cofradia, fushionless, harfen

1. **cofradia (koe-fruh-DEE-uh) (noun):** Roman Catholic laymen in Mexico and Central America who take responsibility for pilgrimages, ceremonies, and the care of religious images. Cofradia also is a town in Honduras.

2. **fushionless (FUSH-uhn-less) (adj.):** Insipid or tasteless; alternatively, to be physically weak or mentally dull. He may be anything but mentally dull, but filmmaker John Waters proudly accepts accolades for being considered one of the most "tasteless" auteurs in cinematic history.

3. **harfen (HARFF-uhn) (verb):** To make constant attempts at improvement. Horatio Alger Jr. became famous in the nineteenth century for his tales of impoverished young men who harfen their way to success.

The fake word is:
harfen

Today, the name Horatio Alger—if recognized at all—suggests a romanticized worldview that is not actually attainable. But in the nineteenth century, people ate up Alger's books like teens reading *Twilight*.

His most popular book, and one that is still in print today, is *Ragged Dick*. As the novel opens, Dick is a homeless, smoking, drinking fourteen-year-old shoeshine boy. He's determined (not harfened) to turn over a new leaf. Some of his customers, recognizing Dick's will to power, befriend the boy, taking him to church, paying him extra, etc.

One day, Dick saves a boy from drowning. In his gratefulness, the boy's father gives Dick a position in his firm. *Voila!* Dick becomes a member of the middle class and forever will be known as Richard Hunter, Esq.

The Trashiest Movie Ever Made?

Despite being forty years old, John Waters's *Pink Flamingos* still has the power to shock. In this darkest of black comedies, Waters seeks to portray practically every taboo imaginable . . . and even some that aren't typically thought of, such as exposing oneself with a large sausage tied to one's privates.

Most famously, the film about "The Filthiest People Alive" ends with its star, Divine, eating actual dog poop. She follows a poodle around until it does its business, picks up the result, throws it in her mouth, and smiles for the camera. Cut! Print! That's a wrap!

dicretinous, bobeche, gomeral

1. **dicretinous (duh-CREET-uh-nuss) (adj.):** Two-faced; given to rapid, unpredictable change. The epitome of a dicretinous character is Two-Face, one of comic book hero Batman's archvillains.

2. **bobeche (boh-BESH) (noun):** A collar on a candle socket to catch wax drippings. When chandeliers used candles, one can only imagine the difficulty servants would have had cleaning and replacing each chandelier's many bobeches.

3. **gomeral (GAHM-uh-rull) (noun):** A simpleton; a fool. Jamaican reggae artist Christopher Harrison was better known as "Simpleton." Simpleton had a 1992 hit with "Coca Cola Bottle Shape."

The fake word is:

dicretinous

Harvey Dent was once Gotham City's district attorney, and he was Batman's friend, helping the Caped Crusader put away legions of bad guys. One day, one of these fiends throws acid in Dent's face, disfiguring one-half of his visage.

Afterward, Dent goes insane. He carries with him a coin. One side is normal, and the other has an "X" scratched on it. Whenever Dent, now going by the moniker "Two-Face," faces a decision, he flips the coin. If the unblemished side comes up, Two-Face does what most would consider the right thing. If the other side comes up, however, he will commit heinous acts.

Reggae's Godfather

Jamaica's Alton Ellis is called the "Godfather of Rocksteady" because he is widely credited with helping to create this musical precursor to reggae. As such, he could also claim a place as the Godfather of Reggae.

Before rocksteady there was ska, a mishmash of traditional Caribbean music, American jazz, and rhythm and blues. Rocksteady slowed down the tempo, leading the way to the more laidback grooves of reggae. The term "rocksteady" comes from an Ellis song called—what else—"Rock Steady."

---

minnesinger, rowdydow, codlerize

1. **minnesinger (MIHN-ih-seeng-uhr) (noun):** One belonging to a class of German lyric poets and musicians flourishing from the twelfth to fourteenth centuries. Three of the most famous are Heinrich von Veldeke, Wolfram von Eschenbach, and Hartmann von Aue.

2. **rowdydow (ROW [rhymes with cowl]-dee-dow) (noun):** Noisy excitement. Think hubbub and hullaballoo. It's almost as much fun to say!

3. **codlerize (KAHD-luhr-ize) (verb):** To make someone or something appear insignificant due to a propensity to repeat a point incessantly. History, literature, and politics are filled with individuals who can't seem to resist revisiting the same point again and again. For example, Herbert Hoover wrote numerous books trying to explain why he wasn't responsible for the onset of the Great Depression, even though it happened during his watch.

The fake word is:
codlerize

If you do it right the first time then there's no need to repeat yourself. To wit: Many people would like to or have tried to write the Great American Novel, and one of the contenders for this unofficial laurel is Harper Lee's *To Kill a Mockingbird*. Published in 1960, Lee's novel is a bildungsroman (coming-of-age story) about a young Southern tomboy whose family becomes embroiled in racial controversy. The novel's characters—Scout, Atticus Finch, "Boo" Radley—have practically attained the stature of living, breathing human beings, especially in light of the Gregory Peck film of the book, which appeared in 1962.

One of literature's enduring mysteries is why Lee never wrote another book. Some have surmised that she didn't write it at all; perhaps, they say, it was actually written by her friend, Truman Capote. Most likely, Lee just realized she had already written one of America's greatest novels.

The Dynamic, Germanic Trio

- Heinrich von Veldeke is purported to be the first writer of the German Low Countries to write in his native language rather than in Latin.
- Wolfram von Eschenbach wasn't just a minnesinger, or lyric poet; he also wrote epics. It is for his epic, *Parzival*, that he is best remembered today.
- Hartmann von Aue is best known for his epic, *Der arme Heinrich*, which influenced later poets such as Longfellow and Rossetti.

---

fatidic, donjon, blistrine

1. **fatidic (fay-TID-ick) (adj.):** Of or relating to prophecy. The latest fatidic "buzz" concerns 2012, but prophecies about the end of the world have existed as long as people have been on this planet.

2. **donjon (DON-juhn) (noun):** A medieval castle's massive inner tower. Not surprisingly, England is the country with the most medieval castles still standing.

3. **blistrine (blih-STREEN) (adj.):** Loud and booming. Any noise at a continuous level of 85 decibels can cause damage to one's hearing.

The fake word is:

blistrine

What was the loudest sound in recorded history? Sources disagree, but here are some of the contenders.

In 1908, a large meteor crashed near the Tunguska River in Russia. Its impact was equivalent to a 1,000-megaton bomb, and it reached the probable decibel level of 300 to 315, enough to kill a human being . . . if he or she weren't vaporized by the meteor's impact, of course.

In 1883, a volcano erupted on the Indonesian island of Krakatoa. Scientists have concluded the noise reached 180 decibels or more, a dozen times louder than the noise of a jet engine at 100 feet away. The eruption could be heard nearly 2,000 miles away.

A "Chilling" Castle

England's Chillingham Castle is said to be the most haunted castle in England.

Built in the late twelfth century, Chillingham Castle was at first a monastery. During medieval times, the castle occupied an important point between two warring nations. As a result, King Edward III gave orders for Chillingham to be fortified, which is when it became an "official" castle.

The building is complete with a medieval torture chamber, which may be why the place is supposedly replete with ghosts. Its most famous specter was the "blue boy," who appeared as a light or shadowy figure tinged that color. Recent renovations uncovered the skeleton of a young boy trapped behind a 10-foot wall. After the skeleton was removed and given a proper burial, the blue boy stopped appearing in Chillingham Castle.

suttee, turt, yare

1. **suttee (suh-TEE) (noun):** The act of a Hindu widow showing devotion to her husband by voluntarily being cremated on the funeral pyre of her husband. Britain officially banned the practice in 1829, but at least forty cases have been reported since India gained independence from Britain in 1947.

2. **turt (TUHRT) (verb):** To make a blast with a car horn. The classic bulb horn—think Harpo Marx—first appeared in America in the early 1900s. It was a "gift" from France.

3. **yare (YAHR) (adj.):** Ready for action; nimble, lively. "Be prepared" has been the Boy Scout motto since 1907.

The fake word is:

turt

The most famous "turt" in television history belonged to the General Lee, the immortal Dodge Charger driven by those good ol' boys on *The Dukes of Hazzard*.

The show lasted from 1979 to 1985 and focused on cousins Bo and Luke Duke. However, most remember either the sexy Daisy Duke and her eponymous cut-off shorts or Bo and Luke's automobile, with its Rebel flag, "01" emblazoned on the side, and horn that played the first twelve notes of "Dixie."

According to television legend, the distinctive horn was not originally planned for the General Lee. While filming in Georgia, a local hotrodder drove by, tooted *his* Dixie horn, and the rest is history. Go through a small Southern town and, sooner or later, you'll hear the "turt" of "Dixie."

Ready for Action!

A likely reason the Boy Scout motto is "Be Prepared" is that the pithy motto shares initials with scouting's founder, Robert Baden-Powell. He explained the motto this way in his book, *Scouting for Boys*:

"The Scout Motto is: BE PREPARED which means you are always in a state of readiness in mind and body to do your DUTY. Be Prepared in Mind by having disciplined yourself to be obedient to every order, and also by having thought out beforehand any accident or situation that might occur, so that you know the right thing to do at the right moment, and are willing to do it."

votruminous, yegg, jubilarian

1. **votruminous** (voh-TROO-muh-nuhss) (adj.): Of or related to man-made objects visible from space. Contrary to popular legend, the Great Wall of China is not a votruminous object.

2. **yegg** (YEGG) (noun): A safecracker; a robber. O. Henry's short story about a yegg, "A Retrieved Reformation," was the source for MGM's first all-talking film.

3. **jubilarian** (joo-buh-LAIR-ee-uhn) (noun): One who celebrates a jubilee. Jubilation "Jubilee" Lee is also one of the amazing X-Men of Marvel Comics fame.

The fake word is:
votruminous

One man-made object that is visible from space is the beam emitting from atop Las Vegas's pyramid-shaped Luxor hotel. The beam shines at 42.3 billion candle power. "Candle power," though no longer a common measure of light, is equal to, as its name suggests, the light from one average candle. According to the hotel-casino's website, an astronaut 10 miles above the Earth could read his or her newspaper by the light of the silvery Luxor. The site also claims that the beam can be seen from a jet plane 250 miles away.

Talking with Yeggs

Alias Jimmy Valentine, based on O. Henry's "A Retrieved Reformation," became MGM's first all-talking picture in 1928. It was actually Hollywood's third film based on the short story by William Sidney Porter, a.k.a. O. Henry. The fact that it was the major studio's first all-talkie makes the film memorable; the plot does not.

The story features hackneyed twists and turns, assumed identities, and a final plot twist at the end. Basically, an expert yegg tries to avoid the law by moving to a small Arkansas town. He falls in love and decides to go legit. Meanwhile, a detective has tracked down Jimmy Valentine.

The town's local bank gets a new "uncrackable" safe, and a small child gets locked into it by accident. Valentine must, of course, make a decision: Should he show off his safecracking skills and get sent to the pokey, or should he save the child? Of course he saves the child. The pursuing detective decides to leave Valentine alone since he only practiced his "art" in order to save someone.

matutinal, plantastine, passacaglia

1. **matutinal** (mach-oo-TINE-uhl) (adj.): Of, relating to, or taking place early in the morning. Coffee made its first inroads as America's morning beverage of choice after England cut tea exports in the wake of the War of 1812.

2. **plantastine** (PLAN-tuh-steen) (adj.): Of or relating to earmarks hidden in some congressional bills. "Pork barrel" did not take on a pejorative sense, in relation to congressional bills, until after the American Civil War.

3. **passacaglia** (pahss-uh-KOLL-yuh) (noun): An ancient Spanish or Italian dance tune. Ironically, the best-known passacaglia was composed by someone neither Spanish nor Italian. Johann Sebastian Bach composed his *Passacaglia and Fugue in C minor* in the early eighteenth century.

The fake word is:

plantastine

The word may be fake, but the practice, of course, isn't. Members of Congress have tried to appropriate federal tax dollars for local projects since there has been a Congress. Sometimes, the projects are beneficial and may even save money over time. And sometimes they're not.

Take Boston's so-called Big Dig, for example. The Big Dig was supposed to take a few miles of an interstate and move it underground to help traffic flow. It wound up costing $14.6 billion, or about $4 billion per mile. In 2006, a portion of the tunnel's ceiling collapsed, killing motorist Milena Del Valle. The project was completed in 2007.

Java, Anyone?

The Indonesian island of Java is the world's most populous island, with 135 million residents. It is home to Jakarta, the country's capital. At one time, it was the nucleus of the Dutch East Indies, which is the origin of the island's association with coffee.

Rice is the country's main crop. During Dutch colonization, the Dutch introduced a number of plants to the island, including coffee. As tea began to lose America's favor and coffee gained it in the late nineteenth and early twentieth century, most coffee originated in Java. As a result, Java has been synonymous with coffee ever since.

---

redingote, asafetida, brignitty

1. **redingote (red-in-GOAT) (noun):** An eighteenth-century, double-breasted coat with collar and wide flat cuffs, designed for travel on horseback. The word is a French alteration of the English words "riding coat."

2. **asafetida (as-uh-FIT-uhd-ee) (noun):** The fetid gum resin of certain members of the carrot family once used in medicine as a panacea. Pharmacies and New Age health food stores still market asafetida for its allegedly miraculous properties.

3. **brignitty (BRIG-nih-tee) (noun):** A small boat, typically motorized, sold as a yacht accessory. The most expensive yacht in the world docks in Dubai and belongs to Russian businessman Roman Abramovich. *The Eclipse* cost $1.2 billion. Yes, that's "billion" with a "b."

The fake word is:
brignitty

What do you get for $1.2 billion? For starters, *The Eclipse* is 528 feet long. By contrast, a football field is 360 feet long.

The Eclipse also has two helipads, in case your rich friends want to fly in. The yacht has eleven staterooms that define sumptuousness, and if you want to dance, then you're set. *The Eclipse* has its own disco. In addition, the yacht has its own submarine and comes complete with a German-manufactured missile defense system (!).

What does Abramovich do in order to be able to afford a yacht like this? The Russian businessman controls a private investment company. He's also owner of England's Chelsea Football Club. And he's only the world's 53rd richest man!

Pass the Asafetida!

If you've never heard of asafetida, then maybe you should check it out:

- Buy it for the gassy people in your life. Asafetida is an anti-flatulent.
- Get it when you're feeling feverish. Researchers outside of America have posited that asafetida helps combat the H1N1 flu strain.
- Find some for those who have trouble breathing. Asafetida supposedly helps combat bronchitis and asthma.
- Try it for the morning after. Asafetida's most controversial alleged use is as an abortifacient (abortion-causing agent).

coulisse, winstead, escadrille

1. **coulisse** (koo-LEES) (noun): A backstage area or hallway. The coulisse should always have a "ghost light" burning, according to theatrical superstition.

2. **winstead** (WIN-stehd) (noun): An ancestral home belonging the same family for more than ten generations. Britain's oldest house, unearthed near North Yorkshire, is 11,500 years old.

3. **escadrille** (EZ-kuh-drill) (noun): A European air command unit typically containing six airplanes. The Lafayette Escadrille, a French Air Service squadron during World War I, was made up largely of American volunteers.

The fake word is:
winstead

North Yorkshire's Star Carr house, the ruins of which were discovered in 2010, has given archaeologists pause.

Most researchers have assumed that England was comprised solely of nomadic hunters in the period immediately following the earth's last Ice Age. Star Carr indicates that these Mesolithic folks may have been homebodies after all.

For example, the site suggests that residents lived with domesticated dogs. It probably had a hearth, and what's more "homey" than a hearth? In addition, archaeologists unearthed a rudimentary wooden platform. The platform's use is unknown, but it demonstrates knowledge of carpentry and the desire to furnish one's pad, Mesolithic style.

Break a Leg, Spirits!

Theater lore is replete with superstitions. For example, one should never wish performers good luck because, paradoxically, that creates bad luck. That's why you tell folks to "break a leg."

One of the most enduring theatrical superstitions is the so-called ghost light. The backstage area of a theater must keep a light burning for its resident ghost. Some contend the light actually wards off ghosts. Others suggest it allows the ghosts to see what's going on, so they won't be tempted to cause pranks in a fit of pique.

But the most likely reason the ghost light exists is so that it won't cause new ghosts. Backstage areas are cluttered and hide orchestra pits. If performers or behind-the-scenes personnel can't see where they're going, then they could fall into something, hit something, or shuffle off this mortal coil in some other "dramatic" way.

---

improvisatore, goliard, haflange

1. **improvisatore (ihm-prahv-uh-zuh-TORE-ee) (noun):**
One who improvises extemporaneous verse. Nowadays, we call these folks rappers.

2. **goliard (GOAL-yuhrd) (noun):** A wandering twelfth- or thirteenth-century student who spent his time writing satire and, basically, goofing off with like-minded people. In essence, these folks were way-ahead-of-their-time hippies.

3. **haflange (HAFF-lihnj) (verb):** To make repairs by using materials dissimilar to those used in the original product, building, etc. The phrase "jury rigged" has been around since the eighteenth century.

The fake word is:
haflange

The use of the word "jury" to indicate something makeshift or temporary pre-dates the concept of "jury rigging" by more than a hundred years. It appears in *A Description of New England* by John Smith, first published in 1616.

If a ship lost its mast, the crew might construct a "joury mast," a mast designed for temporary use. The word "joury" comes from *jour*, the French word for "day." Some have also theorized that the word "jury" comes from the Latin *adjutare*, meaning to aid. Thus, to "jury rig" something is to construct a temporary aid.

Peace, Man!

The word "hippie" is likely a shortened version of the word "hip-ster," which developed in the 1940s and was used to describe the "beatniks" who began to flourish in New York City in the 1950s. The word "beatnik" was coined by *San Francisco Chronicle* reporter Herb Caen in 1958.

Caen took the word "beat," which Jack Kerouac (and others) used to describe his generation and added the diminutive "nik" to it in honor of the recently launched *Sputnik I. Sputnik* was the world's first artificial satellite, and when the Soviet Union launched it, the space race really heated up.

---

plimous, dumka, wyvern

1. **plimous (PLY-muss) (adj.):** Of or relating to material used to fill car seats. The plimous material in many of Henry Ford's early cars was Spanish moss. Supposedly, as a result, many car buyers wound up with mysterious, itchy bumps, caused by bites from the tiny organisms still residing in the moss after it was placed inside the seats.

2. **dumka (DUHM-kuh) (noun):** A Slavic folk ballad that alternates between a melancholy and jubilant tone. Mostly it's depressing, though, so you could think of it as the foundation of emo.

3. **wyvern (WHY-vuhrn) (noun):** A two-legged, winged creature resembling a dragon. Wyverns make an appearance in Dante's *Inferno*. As Dante descends into the eighth circle of Hell, he is aided by Geryon, a fearsome giant mentioned in Greek mythology. Dante's Geryon has the body of a wyvern. He helps Dante and his companion, the poet Virgil, enter the Circle of Fraud.

The fake word is:

plimous

Nothing's more Southern than Spanish moss, right? It hangs from ancient oaks, giving Dixie timelessness and occasional sublimity. The words "Southern gothic" and "Spanish moss" are like two sides of the same coin.

The plant's name, however, is misleading. Spanish moss isn't Spanish. It's not moss either. It's an epiphyte, or air plant. Air plants grow on other plants, but they don't steal nutrients from them. They get all they need from the air and the rain. The connection between the plant and the Spanish is unclear. Perhaps Spanish moss is so-called because it flourishes in Florida, which was explored and settled by the Spanish.

Sad Music for Suburban Teens

Washington, D.C.'s, 1980's punk scene spawned the very first "emo" bands. The name was a truncated version of "emotional hardcore," which was used to describe the music. It was still loud (hence, "hardcore"), but it also had a heart. It was less political than emotional.

By the turn of this century, emo became mainstream, thanks to such bands as Jimmy Eat World and Dashboard Confessional. The word also broke free of its music-specific roots to describe the (mostly) young people who listened to it. The typical emo kid wears black, looks sad all the time, and is full to the brim of suburban angst.

moffette, lycanthral, nosology

1. **moffette** (moh-FET) (noun): A vent in the Earth that issues carbon dioxide, nitrogen, and oxygen. A NASA-supported program determined that the world's deepest hydrothermal vent is some 3.5 miles below the surface of the Caribbean Sea, in an underwater ridge called the Mid-Cayman Rise.

2. **lycanthral** (lie-CAN-thruhl) (adj.): Madness-causing. Another name for a werewolf is a lycanthrope.

3. **nosology** (no-SAHL-uh-jee) (noun): The medical science branch that deals with disease classification. Typically, diseases are classified either by their source cause (etiology) or by the mechanism that sparks the disease (pathogenesis). Nosology isn't always an exact science because the reasons a disease pops up aren't always clear.

The fake word is:

lycanthral

Long before he became a patriarch and a guardian angel, Michael Landon suffered from lycanthropy. American International Pictures, an independent movie studio, enjoyed one of its greatest successes with 1957's *I Was a Teen-age Werewolf*. In the film, troubled teen Tony Rivers (Landon) realizes he has anger-management issues and goes to a hypnotherapist for help. Through the magic of B-movie plot points, the evil therapist instead turns Tony into a werewolf.

The evil doctor's plan (which isn't very clear) backfires when Tony kills him and his assistant before being shot to death by police.

Some twenty years later, the grown-up Landon became "Pa" Ingalls on *Little House on the Prairie* and then the star of *Touched by an Angel*. Oh, and some thirty years after Landon's "lycanthral" transformation, the movie *Teen Wolf* was released. This time, a teenager becoming a werewolf was played strictly for laughs.

The Crack of Life

Did life on Earth originate in deep sea vents like that found in the Mid-Cayman Rise? German chemist, Gunter Wachtershauser thinks so, and other scientists have agreed he might be right.

Wachtershauser's iron-sulfur world theory posits that amino-acid synthesis occurring deep in the Earth's crust may have been shot out into the sea through a thermal vent. Once in the cooler waters and among iron-rich minerals, the acids could have formed basic, living cells. Over time, these cells developed into larger and larger living beings.

colph, zoophilous, interdigitate

1. **colph** (KAHLFF) (noun): An indeterminate pause in music. Although not a colph as such, "4'33"," by experimental composer John Cage, may be the most famous example of this term. For the piece, Cage would merely lift the lid of his piano and pause for four minutes and thirty-three seconds. The "music" was the coughing and stirring of the audience, ambient sirens outside, the dropping of programs, etc. Consequently, the "piece" was different every time it was "performed."

2. **zoophilous** (zoh-AHFF-uh-luss) (adj.): Having an attraction to, or preference, for animals. This is not to be confused with "zoophily," which is a form of pollination by which pollen is transferred by animals.

3. **interdigitate** (in-tuhr-DIJJ-uh-tate) (verb): Becoming interlocked, like the fingers of folded hands. Even though the fingers are not completely interdigitate, you can find the world's largest praying hands in Tulsa, Oklahoma. They're 60 feet tall and weigh 30 tons.

The fake word is:
colph

Almost from the time he began composing, John Cage tried to break with traditional Western music. He worked with so-called prepared pianos, for example. Cage would literally take objects and place them on the strings of his piano so that they would emit odd noises when he played the keys.

After being turned on to the *I Ching*, however, Cage found his principal direction. This seminal work of Chinese philosophy describes a symbol system one can use to identify order in chance events. Typically, it is used for divination, foretelling the future, but Cage used it to create aleatory—or chance-based—music.

Give Me That Old Time Religious Cheese

If you like your religion kitschy and huge, then America has what you're looking for!

Tulsa, as noted, is where you can find the world's largest praying hands, and it's also the home of the (in)famous Oral Robert's prayer tower. The tower is on the site of Oral Roberts University.

Just off Interstate 40 near Groom, Texas, one can find the world's largest cross. Motorists can see the 190-foot cross from as many as 20 miles away. More than one hundred welders put together this steel monument to God (and religious kitsch).

And finally, if you're into the Ten Commandments, then God commands you to visit Murphy, North Carolina. That's where you'll find the Church of God of Prophecy's 300-foot-wide Ten Commandments, which is said to be the world's largest. The impressive structure, built into a hillside and first revealed to the flock in 1945, can supposedly be seen from space!

---

brannigan, variola, norphite

1. **brannigan** (BRAN-ih-guhn) (noun): A drinking spree, or a squabble resulting from a drinking spree. According to folk legend, you can tell whether you're in the West or the East based on barroom fights. If you're in the East, fighters will go outside for their brannigan. If you're in the West, look out—brawlers will stay in the bar!

2. **variola** (vair-ee-OH-luh) (noun): A viral disease marked by pustular eruption. Smallpox is one of the best examples.

3. **norphite** (nor-FITE) (noun): Glass-like material often used in knickknacks. The glass menagerie of Tennessee Williams's eponymous *The Glass Menagerie* likely is made of norphite.

The fake word is:

norphite

Laura Wingfield's glass menagerie probably is just that: glass. The young girl is the fragile center of Williams's 1944 play, which critics consider one of Williams's most autobiographic. Presumably, since his given name is Thomas, Williams is Tom Wingfield.

Williams adopted "Tennessee" from his father, who descended from east Tennessee families. Perhaps Williams thought this would bring him closer to his old man, who disapproved of him for being sickly and effeminate. Cornelius Williams wanted a robust, hearty, "manly" son. While his father disapproved of him, Williams's mother, Edwina, doted on him, but she spent much of her life unhappy and peevish because her life was not as full of Southern gentility as she would have wished.

But Williams transmuted a dysfunctional family into gold. He won just about any award you can think of for his dramas, before dying in 1983 at the age of seventy-one.

A Pox upon You!

At its height, smallpox was one of history's most heinous killers. In the closing years of the eighteenth century, for example, 400,000 Europeans died each year from the disease, which first appeared in humans around 10,000 B.C.

European explorers brought latent forms of the disease with them and may have been responsible for killing 80 to 90 percent (!!) of Indians in lands where smallpox was nonexistent.

Fortunately, a major vaccination campaign during the second half of the twentieth century has eradicated smallpox. The last naturally occurring case was recorded in 1977 in Somalia.

zizith, bastale, fauvism

1. **zizith (TSIT-suhs) (noun):** Fringes or tassels worn by Jewish males on ceremonial or traditional clothing as commanded in Deuteronomy and Numbers. As part of his effort to follow all the rules of the Bible, author A. J. Jacobs began to wear zizith. Prior to attempting a fully biblical life, Jacobs wrote about his successful effort to read an entire set of encyclopedias from cover to cover.

2. **bastale (buh-STALE) (adj.):** Of or relating to certain circus performers. The first "modern" circus was under the direction of Philip Astley, who performed in England in 1768. Astley's circus specialized in horse-riding tricks.

3. **fauvism (FOE-viz-uhm) (noun):** Painting characterized by vivid colors and free treatment of form, typified by Matisse. Matisse, championed by Gertrude Stein just like Pablo Picasso, is, like Picasso, considered one of the most important artists of the twentieth century.

The fake word is:
bastale

One man's name continues to be synonymous with the circus: P. T. Barnum. Of course, Barnum was more than just a circus pioneer. He also fooled thousands with his hoaxes and is credited with coining the saying, "There's a sucker born every minute."

Phineas Taylor Barnum's first hoax, introduced in 1842, was the so-called Feejee Mermaid. This odd-looking mummified creature actually was comprised of the head of a monkey sewn onto the body of a fish.

Barnum always contended that hoaxes like the Feejee Mermaid were simply designed to attract customers to his legitimate exhibits. Barnum went around the world to find unusual people and artifacts, and eventually he opened his own museum. He didn't laugh at "suckers." In fact, he devoted a portion of his career to debunking people who made money solely on fakery, especially those in the burgeoning "spiritualist" movement. Barnum offered the then-extraordinary sum of $500 to any medium who could prove contact with the dead. No one ever got the cash.

The First Encyclopedia Salesman?

Pliny the Elder, a Roman statesman living in the first century A.D., wrote what is considered the first encyclopedia. The *Naturalis Historia* contained thirty-seven chapters, which included information about medicine, architecture, natural history, geology, and pretty much any other subject that caught his interest. In addition to his own hands-on experience, Pliny the Elder gave "props" to 2,000 different works by 200 different authors for the contents of his book, which contained some 20,000 facts.

---

hegira, keratosis, tretchy

1. **hegira (hih-JEYE-ruh) (noun):** A journey undertaken to escape from a dangerous or undesirable situation. Think the Israelites. Think "let my people go."

2. **keratosis (ker-uh-TOE-suhss) (noun):** An area of skin that is overgrown with horny tissue. Keratosis, which isn't pretty to look at, is associated with sun worshipers.

3. **tretchy (TRETCH-ee) (adj.):** Extremely sensitive, as skin or feelings. Once upon a time, tretchy folks were simply considered neurotic and annoying. Since the 1990s, they've been lauded as "highly sensitive," suggesting acuity not available to the average person.

The fake word is:

tretchy

They may not be tretchy, but there is a semi-famous Detroit band that can claim to be high-strung. That's because the group's name is, well, The High Strung.

Singer/guitarist Josh Malerman met drummer Derek Berk at Michigan State Unviersity in the late 1990s. After a move to New York, some lineup changes, and synthesis with another band, The High Strung were formed. The group belongs to the neo-garage band genre, popularized by groups like The White Stripes and The Strokes.

Let My People Go

Whatever knowledge most people have of the Israelite's exodus is likely to come not from the Bible but from Cecil B. DeMille's 1956 epic, *The Ten Commandments*. The film, starring Charlton Heston, was actually a remake of DeMille's 1923 silent movie of the same name. Here are a few of the differences between the Bible and the epic:

- In the film, the pharaohs are named. In the Bible, they aren't.
- In the film, the young Moses is a military hero. This aspect of his career does not appear in the Bible.
- In the Bible, Moses has an undetermined speech impediment, which Heston's Moses does not have.
- In the Bible, the reception of the Ten Commandments is a public event, not the private event depicted in the film.
- Finally, in the Old Testament, the pharaoh's army slaughters Israelite children simply by throwing them into the sea. In the film, swords and bloodshed are more akin to the way Herod slaughtered innocents in the New Testament.

lobbygow, patagium, loist

1. **lobbygow (LAHB-ee-gow) (noun):** An errand boy. One of modern literature's most famous errand boys is Sammy Glick of Budd Schulberg's *What Makes Sammy Run?*

2. **patagium (puh-TAY-jee-uhm) (noun):** The fold of skin connecting a flying squirrel's fore and hind limbs that allows it to "fly." Animation's most famous flying squirrel, Rocket J. Squirrel, was "born" in 1959. Rocket is better known as "Rocky" and is almost never separated from his dull-witted moose friend Bullwinkle.

3. **loist (LOYST) (verb):** To dream of or write about an imaginary paradise. Literature, art, and film are filled with imaginary paradises such as Brigadoon and Shangri-La.

The fake word is:

loist

Loist doesn't exist but these fantastical places do:

- Shangri-La appears in James Hilton's 1933 novel, *Lost Horizon*, which was made into a film by Frank Capra in 1937.
- Alan Jay Lerner and Frederick Loew's *Brigadoon* first appeared on Broadway in 1947. It was made into a film in 1954 and is probably being performed right now in one of your local high schools.
- Avalon, the mythical place and not the Toyota model, first appeared in 1136 in Geoffrey of Monmouth's pseudo-historical *Historia Regum Brittaniae*.
- Utopia was created by Sir Thomas More in 1516.

He's a Sammy Glick

Sammy Glick begins his Hollywood career as a lobbygow but winds up becoming a powerful screenwriter. He is successful because he jumps on any and every opportunity for advancement and doesn't care whom he has to step on in the process. That's why, occasionally, a backstabbing opportunist is even today alluded to as a "Sammy Glick."

Schulberg's 1941 novel skewers Hollywood, which may explain why it was gleefully adapted into a Broadway musical—but has yet to appear as a feature film. The play first opened along the Great White Way in 1964, with Steve Lawrence in the title role.

fleenor, adytum, quadrivium

1. **fleenor** (FLEE-nuhr) (noun): A small, private jet. The celebrity set has been cruising about in fleenors since at least the 1920s.

2. **adytum** (AD-uh-tuhm) (noun): The innermost sanctum of an ancient temple, typically open only to priests. Adytum is also the name of a Canadian Death Metal band.

3. **quadrivium** (kwah-DRIHV-ee-uhm) (noun): The upper division of medieval universities' seven liberal arts, consisting of arithmetic, music, geometry, and astronomy. The goal of studying the quadrivium was to prepare oneself for the serious study of philosophy, which then had more to do with science and now has more to do with college kids who don't really want to get jobs after graduation.

The fake word is:

fleenor

One of the most famous private jets is *The Starship*, used for God only knows what decadent purposes by rock bands.

The Starship was a United Airlines Boeing 720B passenger jet, originally purchased by teen idol Bobby Sherman and his manager. They leased the jet to rock bands in the mid-1970s. Most famously, *The Starship* was the home in the sky of famously profligate band Led Zeppelin, which used it during its 1973 and 1975 tours. Frighteningly, drummer John Bonham acted as co-pilot for part of the trip. Bonham was known for his drinking binges and, ultimately, died from one of them. (Now, *that's* who you want in the driver's seat!)

A Short History of Death Metal

Death Metal first began blasting out of teenage headphones and speakers in the mid-1980s. Kids loved for the same reason they always love obnoxious music: it pisses off their parents! It even attracted the wrath of then-Sen. Al Gore's wife, Tipper.

Death Metal features heavy distortion, multiple basses because the sound should be deep and dark, thrashing drums, and vocals sometimes described as "Cookie Monster" vocals, though that probably doesn't please the folks who live on Sesame Street. Cookie Monster grunts and growls and is barely comprehensible, and this describes Death Metal vocals as well.

Bands that practice the fine art of Death Metal include the above-mentioned Adytum, as well as Slayer, Kreator, Celtic Frost, and Venom.

cembalo, ravelant, lancinate

1. **cembalo (KEM-buh-low) (noun):** Another name for a harpsichord. The harpsichord was invented during the Middle Ages and held sway for hundreds of years until it was obscured by that upstart, the piano.

2. **ravelant (RAHV-uh-luhnt) (adj.):** Of or relating to suspended animation. Contrary to popular belief, Walt Disney is not currently in a ravelant condition.

3. **lancinate (LANT-suh-nate) (verb):** To pierce or stab. Lances, or at least long pointy sticks, as every viewer of an old "sword and sandal" epic" can attest, were mainstays of the Romans as well as medieval knights. Today, they've morphed into javelins.

The fake word is:
ravelant

Since Walt Disney's death in 1966, the legend has persisted that he was put into suspended animation in order to be "thawed out" and "fixed" once medical science figured out a cure for Disney's lung cancer. In fact, most people have "heard" that Disney's body resides somewhere far below the Pirates of the Caribbean ride.

All of this is nonsense, of course, but it makes one wonder how such a rumor got started in the first place. Perhaps it was the fact that Disney's robotic creations (which he called animatronics)—President Lincoln, singing and dancing bears, etc.—are so lifelike that people believe he and his engineers can create miracles.

You Play the What?

The harpsichord isn't the only musical instrument left behind by progress.

- The therodo was a large, bass lute with many strings. The therodo was pretty much kaput by 1750.
- The intonarumori were large boxes that produced electronic noises. They were created around 1917 by Futurist artist and writer Luigi Russolo, best remembered today for being the author of *The Art of Noises*.
- The telharmonium, created by Thaddeus Cahill in 1897, was another early electronic instrument that is no longer used. It was an early version of a synthesizer but quite ungainly.
- The unpleasantly named bladder pipe was a simplified bagpipe, used during medieval times. Was it the name? Was it the fact that most people hate bagpipes?

---

turnivie, salariat, bibcock

1. **turnivie (TUHR-nuh-vee) (verb):** To make nervous or uncertain. A recent survey undertaken by the American Diabetes Association indicates that people are most afraid of dying in a plane crash. Getting a disease, the fear most likely to happen, concerned only five percent of those surveyed.

2. **salariat (suh-LAHR-ee-uht) (noun):** The class of salaried workers. The word is typically used as contrast to the wage-earning class.

3. **bibcock (BIB-kahk) (noun):** A faucet with a bent-down nozzle. Mixer taps, which can mix together hot and cold water, were invented in 1880.

The fake word is:
turnivie

There are plenty of things that could bring on turnivie (if it were real, that is). The annual risk of being killed in a plane crash is one in eleven million. The annual risk of being killed in a car crash is one in 5,000, and the likelihood of dying from heart disease is one in 400. Yet, fear of flying tops the survey. Why?

As far as driving is concerned, most of us drive far more often than we fly. If we manage 4,999 times to get into our cars, negotiate traffic, and fiddle around to grasp objects just out of reach, we're not going to be likely to think, "Oh, this is the time that doing these things will kill me."

And as for heart disease, all of us, on some level, know we're possibly contributing to an early demise each time we chow down on wieners at the ball game. However, we eat those tasty little carcinogenic suckers time and again without dropping dead. So, as Alfred E. Neuman would say, "What, me worry?"

Taking Care of Business

In America, the salariat is considered a higher class than that of the hourly wage earner. True, "salary" conjures up images of jobs with a lot of responsibility and with benefits, but hourly wages have their benefits as well.

For one thing, hourly workers know exactly how many hours they will toil. If they do work more than their prescribed hours, then they are eligible for overtime, which usually pays time-and-a-half. Salaried workers typically are expected to work overtime without any extra compensation.

---

demulcent, telpher, alcatine

1. **demulcent (dih-MULL-suhnt) (adj.):** Soothing. Everything from classical music to a warm bath to the sight of meat (!) can be considered demulcent for human beings.

2. **telpher (TELL-fur) (noun):** A car suspended from and running on aerial cables. Amusement parks sometimes employ telphers in their "dark rides."

3. **alcatine (AL-kuh-teen) (adj.):** Given to drunkenness. In 1990, 51 percent of traffic fatalities were related to alcohol. The number, fortunately, has dropped since. In 2008, for example, alcohol was connected to 37 percent of traffic fatalities.

The fake word is:

alcatine

One of America's "favorite" drunks is Otis Campbell, a stalwart of *The Andy Griffith Show*. Actor Hal Smith portrayed Otis regularly from 1960 to 1967 but stopped appearing as the show ended its run. Too many tongues were wagging over the concept of a "loveable" drunk. In 1986's *Return to Mayberry*, Otis reappeared. The show emphasized that Otis had been sober for years, and was Mayberry's beloved ice cream man. According to Griffith himself, Smith was a teetotaler who had never had a drink in his life. Smith died in 1994.

Laughter in the Dark

Dark rides, called ghost trains in England, once were staples of amusement parks. They've lost ground in recent years to ever-more-thrilling roller coasters and other types of "action" rides. A typical dark ride, as its name suggests, takes riders through dark tunnels, past scenes designed to excite, amuse, and/or frighten.

One early dark ride was Futurama, a popular exhibit at the 1939 New York World's Fair. The ride, sponsored by General Motors and designed by Norman Bel Geddes, took riders into the fantastic world of the future . . . circa 1959–1960. The ride was accurate in some ways. While we still don't have automated highways, we do have hectares of sprawling suburbs and roadways that crisscross the United States.

Futurama II appeared at the 1964 New York World's Fair. This time, the ride took crowds into 2024. As that year approaches, we still do not have lunar vacations.

guimpe, tintatious, meatus

1. **guimpe (GAMP) (noun):** A blouse worn under a jumper. This should not be confused with "gimp," which refers to narrow ornamental trim used in sewing or embroidery.

2. **tintatious (tin-TAY-shuss) (adj.):** Of or relating to sounds not capable of being detected by human beings without special equipment. Human beings have a hearing range from 20 to 20,000 hertz. Dogs, on the other hand, have a range that extends to 60,000 hertz.

3. **meatus (mee-ATE-us) (noun):** A natural body passage. Examples include the ear canal, the nose, and the urinary meatus.

The fake word is:

tintatious

If you're a fan of The Beatles' seminal 1967 release, *Sgt. Pepper's Lonely Hearts Club Band*, then you may be dismayed to learn you've not heard all of it. That's okay. No human being ever has.

As some sort of joke, the Fab Four ended "A Day in the Life," considered by many the group's greatest song, with a dog whistle. Apparently, they just liked the idea that someday, somewhere, someone would be listening to the album with his or her dog and then wonder what the heck had gotten into Fido!

Now, That's a Jumper!

A jumper isn't just an article of women's clothing. It's also a religious term.

The Welsh Methodist revival brought life back to Christianity in Wales during the eighteenth century. Charismatic preachers such as Griffith Jones and Howell Harris converted thousands. People who attended worship meetings would get so excited that they would jump up and down for joy; hence, the name "jumpers," typically used in a pejorative manner by outsiders.

The Welsh Methodist revival began to peter out as the eighteenth century ended and many of its most exciting ministers died.

---

lloyful, undine, enuresis

1. **lloyful (LOY-full) (adj.):** Filled with enthusiasm, especially for new cultural advancements. The World Wide Web, arguably humankind's most recent life-shifting cultural advancement, was predicted in a science fiction story of the 1940s.

2. **undine (UHN-deen) (noun):** A water nymph. An undina was a prehistoric, lobe-finned fish. The most famous undine is probably the star of Hans Christian Andersen's "The Little Mermaid," made into a popular Disney film in 1989.

3. **enuresis (en-you-REE-suhs) (noun):** The involuntary discharge of urine. Kimberly-Clark first introduced Depends in 1984. Initially, they were unisex. A gender-specific variation was introduced in 2009.

The fake word is:
lloyful

Astounding Science Fiction's March 1946 issue included the quite-prescient story, "A Logic Named Joe," by Will F. Jenkins.

In the story, "logics" are akin to personal computers. One of them, named Joe, figures out how to send information around in "the tank." The tank is very similar to today's servers. Other logics pick up on Joe's information and begin sending out their own. In no time at all, logics are offering "assistance" in the form of sex advice to children and ways to carry out the perfect murder.

Consequently, logics and their new form of communication wreak havoc on the world. (Some would argue that the World Wide Web has done the same thing.)

Lost in Space

In 2007, astronaut Lisa Marie Nowak figured out a new use for undergarments designed to combat enuresis. In an effort to confront a woman she considered a rival for the affections of another astronaut, Nowak drove from Houston, Texas, to Orlando, Florida. In order to reach her rival at the airport, Nowak stopped as little as possible.

One way to curb pit stops was to use incontinence undergarments and just take care of business in them. This detail became the one most readers of the bizarre story remember best. Nowak confronted her rival at the airport and spritzed her with pepper spray. As a result, Nowak was charged with battery and attempted kidnapping.

---

intrestinate, hippocrepian, floccinaucinihilipilification

1. **intrestinate (in-TRESS-tuh-nut) (adj.):** Of or related to something that evokes an immediate reaction. The view over the Grand Canyon, for example, or a couple in the grip of love at first sight . . . or a giant vat of snakes could all be considered intrestinate.

2. **hippocrepian (his-uh-KREP-ee-an) (adj.):** Shaped like a horseshoe. There is an order of freshwater bryozoa (little tiny animals) whose tentacles are shaped like horseshoes. The word derives from "hippos," the Greek for "horse" and "krepis," which in Greek means "shoe."

3. **floccinaucinihilipilification (FLAH-si-NAH-si-ni-HIL-i-PIL-i-fi-KAY-shun) (noun):** Considering something of no importance. First used in the eighteenth century, this word is one of the longest in the English language.

The fake word is:

intrestinate

Is there a more famous example of love at first sight than that of Juliet and her Romeo? People tend to forget, however, that, as the romantic play opens, Romeo is in love with someone else. Rosaline, who has no lines in the play, exists just long enough to make Romeo sad before he meets Juliet and falls in love, "for real" this time.

In 2004, researchers at Ohio State University appeared to prove that love—or at least like—at first sight may actually exist. Researchers paired 164 students in a "speed friendship" process. The findings were that pairs who developed friendships had made connections almost immediately upon meeting.

Getting Peevish

Pet peeves are those seemingly unimportant situations we confront each day that, despite our better judgment, really upset us. Our pet peeves emerge from the dissonance between what we think people should do versus what some people actually do. One of my other books focuses completely on the subject of "unwritten rules" people should follow, and here are just a few examples.

- One should always put one's shopping cart in the "cart corral" after unloading it. Otherwise, the cart could be directed into someone else's car by a wayward breeze.
- One should always take advantage of the "mercy flush" because your effluvia really does stink.
- One should never take the last cookie/doughnut/ice cream bar.
- One should never sing or whistle off-key around other people, especially when one is at work.

---

fluncability, bumf, honorificabilitudinity

1. **fluncability (FLUNCE-uh-bill-uh-tee) (noun):** Approaching the state of flunking a class. The word's root, "flunk," is a derivation of the word "funk," which in early Scottish dialect meant "to fail due to panic."

2. **bumf (buhmf) (noun):** Boring, unwanted printed stuff we get in the mail—from the government, mail-order houses, catalogs. It comes from the term "bum fodder," meaning toilet paper.

3. **honorificabilitudinity (HO-nor-i-fi-CAB-il-i-tu-DIN-i-tee) (noun):** Having the quality of being honorable. The eighteenth-century New England astronomer Nathaniel Bowditch learned to spell this word in his school in Salem, Massachusetts, which gives an idea of the things people were learning back then.

The fake word is:

fluncability

Compared to much of the rest of the world, the United States appears to have many students demonstrating "fluncability."

A recent comprehensive study compared American students' performance in science and math with the performance of students in thirty other industrialized countries. The results were not particularly encouraging. Science scores were lower than the average of sixteen other countries. Math scores were lower than the average of twenty-four (!) other countries.

Maybe we should just ship our students off to Finland. The Scandinavian country—that most Americans regardless of age probably couldn't pick out on a map—ranked top in both math and science.

Hanging Out in Salem

Salem's execution of presumed witches is pretty mild, really. From 1300 to 1600, the entire continent of Europe was in the grip of "witch fever," finding Satan's power everywhere. Hundreds of thousands of people were executed. The witchcraft trials in Salem occurred from 1692 to 1693, and only twenty "witches" were executed, most by hanging.

Nonetheless, the Salem trials continue to hold sway over the popular imagination, and playwright Arthur Miller is partly responsible. Miller's 1953 play, *The Crucible*, offers a semifictional account of the events in Salem. To this day, few students ever get out of high school without reading and/or viewing the drama.

---

intromit, Mastingerize, usufruct

1. **intromit (in-truh-MIT) (verb):** To enter or send. The word's first recorded use of the word dates back to 1600.

2. **Mastingerize (MAST-in-juh-rize) (verb, usually capitalized):** To submit to tortures based on a victim's personal fears, named for Dr. Albert Mastin, a psychiatrist who pioneered research in the field of fear.

3. **usufruct (YOU-suh-frukt) (noun):** A legal term meaning the right to use someone else's property, as long as you don't destroy it. When you rent an apartment from a landlord, you are enjoying usufruct of his property.

The fake word is:
Mastingerize

There is no fear researcher named Albert Mastin, but a man named Bill Tancer who has become a researcher of people's online behavior learns about more than just what people buy; he also learns something about human behavior.

For one study, Tancer sought to learn what people (at least people who surf the Internet) fear most. Here is his top ten list: flying, heights, clowns, intimacy, death, rejection, people, snakes, success, and driving.

The American Dream

The words "the American Dream" still bring to mind a picture of white picket fences, a lovely suburban home, smiling children, and a dog in the backyard. But the dream has changed over the years.

Most trace the American Dream to Thomas Jefferson's *Declaration of Independence* and specifically to the portion of it that guarantees "life, liberty, and the pursuit of happiness." In Jefferson's time, most would have considered owning huge tracts of land the American Dream. Those same people would have taken those huge chunks of land and toiled to make farms out of them. People today are not as fond of the concept of "toil."

During the nineteenth century, the American Dream called immigrants to mind. Many people came from many places to find better lives for themselves, free from despots, overcrowding, and grim social conditions. Home ownership became the chief symbol of America's opportunities. By the twentieth century, the American Dream began to focus on the quality of having more than one's neighbor. Home ownership was still a part of it—as long as your house was the biggest on the block.

---

caitiff, agraffe, nordyl

4. **caitiff (KAY-tif) (noun):** A coward. This medieval word comes from the old French and was regularly hurled by knights at one another as they jousted for their ladies' honor.

5. **agraffe (uh-GRAF) (noun):** The wire that holds the cork on a champagne bottle. The word comes from the French "agrafer," which means to hook or fasten.

6. **nordyl (NOR-duhl) (noun):** Similar to "idyll," which refers to poetry about life in the country, "nordyl" refers to poetry about the joys of life in cold climates. Ancient Greek poet Theocritus wrote many idylls in the third century. William Cullen Bryant wrote many nordyls during the nineteenth century.

The fake word is:

nordyl

William Cullen Bryant didn't write any nordyls because they don't exist, but he was once considered America's greatest poet. A large chunk of his reputation rests on the poem "Thanatopsis."

"Thanatopsis" (1817) is a meditation on death, and it's also a neologism, coined from the Greek words "thanatos" (death) and "-opsis" (sight). Bryant claimed to have written most of the poem as a teenager, but some of his (possibly jealous) contemporaries swore he stole the poem from foreign sources and simply tweaked it a bit.

In its day, when death trumped medical science regularly, "Thanatopsis" was a crowd-pleaser. Today, the poem strikes us as morbid. Here are its opening lines: "Yet a few days, and thee, / The all-beholding sun, shall see no more, / In all his course; nor yet in the cold ground, / Where thy pale form was laid."

Courtly Love?

Courtly love, which we associate with bold knights in days of old may not even have existed. Most of what we think about when we think about courtly love is rooted in literature of the romantic period and the Victorian era.

If it did exist, it sounds pretty awful. Basically, the idea was that a knight would settle his affections on a noblewoman. She would be his muse, the bedrock of every lance thrust. But no sex ever took place. This love was supposed to be ideal. There was an erotic component to it, but the eroticism was sublimated completely and intertwined somehow with a spiritual element.

It's no wonder the concept of courtly love is associated with those notoriously repressed Victorians.

---

plagium, defenster, moquelumnan

1. **plagium** (PLAY-jee-uhm) (noun): Kidnapping. Even though it happened in 1932, the plagium of aviation pioneer Charles Lindbergh's young son remains a part of America's collective cultural psyche.

2. **defenster** (dee-FENCE-tuhr) (noun): One who builds windows. Louis Comfort Tiffany remains the gold standard for defensters worldwide.

3. **moquelumnan** (moke-uh-LUHM-nuhn) (noun): A Native American language family in the western United States, also known as Miwok. Miwok, and four other language families, is typically brought under an umbrella grouping called Penutian.

The fake word is:

defenster

Often imitated—just look at the plastic lighting fixtures that hang over the tables of many restaurants—there was only one Louis Comfort Tiffany.

This stained-glass maestro began his career as a painter but became interested in glassmaking while still a young man. He sought to merge the two artistic pursuits. His first major commission was the interior design of the Mark Twain House in Connecticut.

But Tiffany was best known for being the guy who brought some fabulosity to the White House. Soon after his election, President Chester Arthur made clear he did not intend to move into the storied residence unless it was decorated properly. Tiffany got the job.

Not So Lucky Lindy

Flying is a common pursuit today, so it's easy to forget the shadow Charles Lindbergh once cast on American culture. Nowadays, he's derided for his Nazi sympathies, and rightly so. However, Lucky Lindy was the king of America for years following his solo trans-Atlantic flight of 1927. Then came one of many crimes considered "The Crime of the Century."

Charles Lindbergh Jr., only twenty months old, was abducted from his family's New Jersey home on March 1, 1932. Two months later, the child's body was found. The cause of death was a skull fracture. Two years later, an illegal German immigrant named Bruno Hauptmann was arrested for the crime, put on trial, and executed for it.

That particular crime of the century also produced one of America's many "Trials of the Century," one the writer H. L. Mencken called "the biggest story since the Resurrection."

lamnation, enneastyle, babouvism

1. **lamnation (LAM-nay-shun) (noun):** The state of being under the influence of marijuana. The word appears throughout the cult classic "educational" film *Reefer Madness*, whenever an "expert" needs to talk to parents about the dangers of marijuana cigarettes.

2. **enneastyle (EN-ee-uh-style) (adj.):** Characterized by nine-rowed columnation. The Parthenon, perhaps the most famous columned ruin in the world, misses being ennastyle by one column.

3. **babouvism (buh-BOO-vihz-uhm) (noun):** A social doctrine espousing egalitarianism and communism, especially as laid out by Francois-Noel Babeuf. Babeuf was ahead of his time. He was active during the French Revolution, and, retroactively, his philosophy has been labeled anarchist, socialist, and communist, even though none of these terms existed during Babeuf's day.

The fake word is:
lamnation

When initially released in 1936, *Reefer Madness* was titled *Tell Your Children*, and it was financed by a religious group. The group's desire was to inform parents of the menace of marijuana, an alternative to alcohol that began gaining prominence during Prohibition.

Exploitation film pioneer Dwain Esper re-cut the film and rereleased it soon after with its new, more "dangerous" sounding title. *Reefer Madness* spent some time on the film circuit and then puffed its last.

It was rediscovered in 1971 by marijuana advocate Keith Stroup, and it quickly became a cult classic on college campuses nationwide. Since then, it has been turned into a musical.

Why is it so popular? Because it is so over the top. Kids in *Reefer Madness* take one or two puffs, and go off to commit rape, manslaughter, and suicide . . . if they don't simply descend into madness.

Parthenon, Take Two!

Leave it to the United States to take a broken-down "famous" building and improve upon it. That's just what happened in Nashville, sometimes known as the "Athens of the South" (even though the South has plenty of other Athens . . . including one in east Tennessee).

Local boosters re-created Greece's crumbling Parthenon to coincide with Tennessee's centennial (1897). The original plaster, wood, and brick building was torn down, and a concrete building put up in its place. That version, which still stands today, was completed in 1931. Unlike the Greek version, Nashville's Parthenon isn't a ruin. It has central heat and air, and it has electric lights. Take THAT, "Athens of the Greece."

hagseed, wrongous, blatitious

1. **hagseed (HAG-seed) (noun):** The children of a witch. American businesswoman Hetty Green gained the unflattering moniker "The Witch of Wall Street" because of her "magical" abilities to make money on Wall Street and for her miserliness. Does that mean her two children were or were not "hagseed?"

2. **wrongous (RAHNG-uhss) (adj.):** Iniquitous, illegal, unlawful. Almost everyone is guilty of a wrongous act from time to time: speeding, jaywalking, talking on his or her cell phone while driving.

3. **blatitious (bluh-TISH-us) (adj.):** Characterized by being blatantly obvious. We love blatitious things because they allow us to feel smarter than other human beings. God, they're dumb, we think. That (situation, affair, etc.) is as plain as the nose on his/her face!

The fake word is:
blatitious

As the Internet gained prominence, it spawned a new superhero: Captain Obvious!

The exact origin of this omnipresent "do-gooder" is unclear, but one thing's blatant: Captain Obvious is everywhere!

The typical way one alludes to this clueless hero is by uttering the statement, "Thank you, Captain Obvious." One says this when someone else has made a blatantly obvious observation, such as, "Well, you really shouldn't have turned on the blender after you dropped your glasses into it." At times, Captain Obvious can be found with his sidekick, "Readily Apparent Boy."

How Do You Know She Is a Witch?

Hetty Green inherited $7.5 million and then made a series of wise investments. Green made most of her money by investing in greenbacks, currency released by the U.S. government after the Civil War. At her death in 1916, Green's personal fortune was between $100 million and $200 million, more than $2 billion today.

She kept most of her fortune due to intense stinginess. When her son broke his leg, Green tried to get him healed at a free clinic (she was recognized). She wore the same underwear until it wore out (!). Green never turned on the heat. She never used hot water. She eschewed fine food for cheap meat pies. She even asked one of her servants to save soap powder by only cleaning the dirtiest parts of her dresses. Green may not have flown on a broom, but she was witch-like nonetheless.

---

morcut, olibanum, wrawl

1. **morcut (MORE-cut) (adj.):** Prone to burst into song. The word, often capitalized, comes from the University of Ohio's Dr. James Morcut, who first diagnosed this psychological disorder in 1952.

2. **olibanum (oh-LIB-uh-nuhm) (noun):** Frankincense. As most people know, olibanum was one of the gifts given by the Magi (the "three wise men" or "three kings") to the baby Jesus. Frankincense was used by Egyptians to create makeup, and it was used later as an ingredient in perfume. The rise of Christianity actually caused a frankincense "panic" because the tree-based product was being dangerously overharvested.

3. **wrawl (ROLE) (verb):** To cry, to howl. Most likely, the word is an example of onomatopoeia.

The fake word is:

morcut

The only time "normal" people burst into song is when they star in musicals. And, like him or loathe him, Andrew Lloyd Webber is one of the most commercially successful composers of all time.

Webber first began working with his lyricist, Tim Rice, in the 1960s. Their first success, *Joseph and the Amazing Technicolor Dreamcoat*, has become a staple of the theater, from Broadway revivals to high school drama clubs.

On a Mott Uh Pee Uh

Pow! Smash! Biff! Boom!

For generations, young people have been introduced to onomatopoeia via comic books and graphic novels. The literary term denotes words that imitate or suggest sounds, and one of its unsung pioneers is cartoonist Roy Crane (1901–1977). The Texan took up cartooning in his teens and created the (at the time) popular syndicated strip, *Wash Tubbs*, in 1924. Tubbs was a nebbish who spent his time looking for treasure in exotic locations.

Along the way, Crane began to introduce "sound effects" to his strip. He used such words as "bam," "pow," and "kersplash" to suggest the sounds of fighting and splashing. Crane also created the characters Captain Easy and Buz Sawyer, which also made extensive use of onomatopoeia. Before long, other cartoonists, comic book authors, and pop artists made use of Crane's innovative techniques.

---

blouwildebeesoog, xarque, nartyl

1. **blouwildebeesoog (BLAU-vill-duh-bay-soak) (noun):** A disease that affects the eyes of sheep. The disease typically causes blindness, and in some cases it leads to the rupture of the affected animal's eyeball.

2. **xarque (SHAR-key) (noun):** A Portuguese variation of charqui, or beef jerky. In 1928, Adolph Levis created a cured-beef sausage. The jars of his product featured an elegant man sporting a top hat and cane. His name? Slim Jim. The rest is snack food history.

3. **nartyl (NAHR-till) (noun):** A small rodent, found typically in the South Seas. Drinking the blood of nartyls is said to produce a mild hallucinogenic effect.

The fake word is:
nartyl

Chances are, if nartyls existed, you would have tried to score some powdered nartyl blood for household huffing. Now that you're a (supposedly) mature adult, we thought we'd clue you in to some of the things your kids might be finding around the house that can create a cheap buzz. Don't let them try this at home!

- Nutmeg. Yes, the stuff you put in apple pies. Swallow enough, and the result is not unlike a marijuana high. The downside, though, is that after the high you'll have an excruciating headache and will throw up everything in your digestive system.
- Whipped cream. Most canisters use nitrous oxide as propellant. A few whiffs of nitrous oxide, the "laughing gas" your dentist uses, remain in the can after the cream is gone.
- Toads. Yes, there is truth to this urban legend, but only if you're using the right toad. The skin and venom of the Colorado River Toad can create a mild high.
- Cough syrup. Copious amounts of cough syrup can get you more than temporary relief from your cold symptoms.

Eww, Gross!

If this book were somehow to fall into the hands of director David Lynch, he might well begin a search for a sheep enduring blouwildebeesoog. The acclaimed director of the surrealistic masterpiece *Eraserhead* and the slightly (but only slightly) more commercial *Blue Velvet* loves to dissect animals and then put the parts together in interesting ways. Just think of the interesting results he could get from the corpse of a sheep with an exploded eyeball.

---

banausic, qualate, venireman

1. **banausic (buh-NOSE-ick) (adj.):** Utilitarian, practical, dull, and menial; or, moneymaking, breadwinning. Getting rich quick, the *sine qua non* of Las Vegas, is decidedly not banausic. That doesn't stop people from flocking there. However, not even Sin City is immune from tough economic times. Suckers only lost $482.7 million in January 2011, compared with a healthier $495 million in January 2010.

2. **qualate (KWAHL-ate) (verb):** To gather historically accurate items for museum displays. If you're a qualator, you spend your days combing through junk and garbage to find just the right table to go behind that wax figure of Lyndon Johnson.

3. **venireman (vuh-NEAR-ee-man) (noun):** A juror. People will sometimes go to tremendous lengths to avoid jury duty. In April 2011, for example, a Brooklyn woman attempted to get out of her civic duty by making a string of racist comments. At first, the judge's punishment was to make the woman serve on juries indefinitely. Later, however, he relented. The woman served her day of jury duty in solitary confinement and then was allowed to go home.

The fake word is:

qualate

Wax museums are just one example of our culture's forgotten "virtual reality of yesterday." When wax likenesses first emerged in the wake of the French Revolution, people flocked to see the "stars" of their day up close and personal. Now, TMZ and other websites bring the famous and infamous into one's house regularly. Nearly gone also are the venerable View-Master and the "Wild West" theme park.

Your Best Bet

While no visit to Las Vegas is particularly banausic, your best chance at beating the house (legally) is to play blackjack at a casino featuring single-deck play. Many casinos on the Strip use multiple decks, which lower your odds. You may have to go to Glitter Gulch or downtown Las Vegas to find single-deck blackjack, which, if played with the right strategy, can give you a slight edge over the house.

flaggate, primuline, ignimbrite

1. **flaggate** (FLAG-ate) (adj.): Resembling or shaped like a flag. "The Star-Spangled Banner" became the United States's national anthem in 1931, which is somewhat ironic. The familiar tune is based on a drinking song, and in 1931 the United States was still in the midst of Prohibition.

2. **primuline** (PRIM-yuh-lean) (noun): A yellow dye. Primuline is fluorescent, and it is "officially" known as Direct Yellow 7.

3. **ignimbrite** (IG-nuhm-brite) (noun): A type of rock formed from volcanic ash. The United States has 169 active volcanoes. According to geology.com, eleven of them have been designated by the United States Geological Survey as "Very High Threat Volcanoes."

The fake word is:

flaggate

America's national anthem is based on the Battle of Fort McHenry, which took place in Baltimore during the War of 1812. The British fired on the fort for twenty-five hours, but Fort McHenry was not severely damaged. On the morning of September 14, 1814, soldiers raised a large United States flag over the fort to replace one that had been damaged by British fire.

The flag had been made a few weeks earlier by Mary Pickersgill and her daughter. It was this flag that Baltimore lawyer/amateur poet Francis Scott Key saw, and he wrote the poem "Defence of Fort McHenry" as a result. Key apparently wrote his poem to the tune of a drinking song called "To Anacreon in Heaven." A Baltimore music store owner put Key's poem and the tune together and called it "The Star-Spangled Banner."

Ready to Blow

Of the eleven extremely volatile volcanoes in the United States, three in particular have scientists on edge.

- Washington's Mount St. Helens, which killed dozens and destroyed some 200 square miles in 1980, could have another major eruption at any time.
- Wyoming's Yellowstone Volcano is approaching eruptive conditions. If it were to go off, it would cover huge portions of the United States with ash and make flying impossible for a lengthy period.
- Washington's Glacier Peak is troubling for other reasons. It hasn't erupted in nearly 2,000 years, but if it were to erupt damage would likely be worse than that caused by Mount St. Helens. In addition, some scientists suggest the volcano is not adequately monitored.

skawmish, orthopter, cynegetic

1. **skawmish (SKAW-mish) (adj.):** A variant of "squeamish," used principally in Great Britain. Chaucer's salty "Miller's Tale" contains the immortal line, "he was somedeel skawmish of fartyng." In other words, "he was freaked out by flatulence."

2. **orthopter (OR-thahp-tuhr) (noun):** A flying machine propelled by the flapping of wings. Since 1991, the energy drink Red Bull has sponsored international "flugtags" ("flying day" in German). These contests urge competitors to create human-powered flying machines. The record is from Flugtag Austria 2000. The winning team created a machine that covered 195 feet before landing.

3. **cynegetic (SIN-uh-jet-ick) (adj.):** Of or relating to hunting. At one time, humans had to hunt to survive. Now it's just an excuse to get drunk with buddies.

The fake word is:
skawmish

In Chaucer's text, the word actually is "squaymous" (not skawmish), which means squeamish.

Coming as it does immediately upon the heels of the chivalrous "Knight's Tale," "The Miller's Tale" is particularly shocking. In it, a student cuckolds his landlord so he can get with his wife by telling him a flood of biblical proportions is imminent. Several twists and turns later, and *another* suitor of the landlord's wife winds up having his ladylove fart in his face. (It's dark, and he thinks he's puckering up toward her face.)

Since this other rival is "squaymous of fartyng he runs off, so the student has the landlord's wife to himself. (And you thought fart jokes were a product of the twentieth century.)

Dangerous Game

One story most high school students are forced to read and often end up actually liking is Richard Connell's "The Most Dangerous Game."

The story first appeared in an issue of *Collier's* in 1924. In it, a famous big game hunter and author of books on hunting named Sanger Rainsford winds up on a mysterious island, which turns out to be the home of a sinister-looking Russian named General Zaroff. Zaroff, as it turns out, is a hunting aficionado, so he recognizes Rainsford.

Zaroff says he had gotten completely fed up with the "ease" of hunting even the most dangerous big game, but he has figured out a new sport—he hunts human beings on his island. Since people can think and reason, they are "the most dangerous game." The title also refers to the "game" of strategy that is the hunt itself.

boomkin, hoy, spumpter

1. **boomkin (BOOM-kin) (noun):** A variant of "bumpkin." "Bumpkin" is a nice word for "redneck."

2. **hoy (HOY) (interjection):** An interjection used to drive farm animals. The word should not be confused with "Oi!", a form of U.K. punk rock that flourished in the 1970s.

3. **spumpter (SPUHM-ter) (noun):** A word carnival workers use instead of the word the rest of us use: "sucker." (Does anyone really think those games are winnable?)

The fake word is:

spumpter

Not all the suckers are the ones trawling the midway for stuffed animals. You might also be a sucker if you invested heavily in the once-mighty Midway Games, Inc., which liquidated its assets following a 2009 bankruptcy filing.

At one time, Midway was the hottest video game company on the planet—with the possible exception of Atari, which also ain't what it used to be. Midway, which started out in the 1950s, paired up with Japanese manufacturers of early video games in the 1970s. It hit it big in 1978 when it distributed the game many Gen Xers still consider the original video game: Space Invaders.

Space Invaders was followed by the immortal Pac-Man and its spin-off, Ms. Pac-Man. Midway moved into the home video game market in 1996, but quickly foundered as newer companies eclipsed them.

Oi! Vey!

Punk, at least the British version, included a lot of art school dropouts and other young people of privilege who seemed to be rebels for the hell of it.

The Oi! movement saw itself as an antidote to advantaged rockers. It was made up of working-class stiffs, skinheads, and other "undesirables" who truly saw no future for themselves. The name came from Cockney Rejects' frontman, Stinky Turner, who would say it while introducing a new song during the group's live shows.

Other Oi! groups include: Angelic Upstarts, The Blood, and Combat 84.

---

spealbone, plithant, gamp

1. **spealbone** (SPEEL-bone) (noun): A shoulder blade used for divination by magicians or medicine men. What's with these "medicine men?" Can't they just buy a Magic 8 Ball like the rest of us?

2. **plithant** (PLITH-uhnt) (adj.): Of or relating to one who reads incessantly. Bibliophiles love books, but plithant individuals read so much that they border on pathological.

3. **gamp** (GAMP) (noun): A large umbrella, named after Sarah Gamp, a character in Charles Dickens's *Martin Chuzzlewit*. Gamp always has a large cotton umbrella with her.

The fake word is:
plithant

Bibliophiles may be considered pathological by their non-bibliophile spouses, but there's no such word as plithant.

Nowadays, one might consider Dickens fans as plithant. High schoolers run in horror from his books, thanking God for sparknotes.com. At one time, though, Dickens was the equivalent of a rock star. His writing, which typically appeared in serial fashion, was waited for with bated breath. When he visited the United States in 1842, he was mobbed by fans.

Keep in mind that the dour man with the receding hairline and unkempt beard who peers out of old photographs doesn't do justice to the young Dickens. If portraits of the time are to be believed, the author wasn't just rock-star popular, he was movie-star handsome.

Better Not Tell You Now

Albert Carter invented the Syco-Seer in 1948. He was inspired to create a divination toy because his mother was a successful clairvoyant in Cincinnati. The first models were encased in clear plastic and attracted the attention of Brunswick Billiards, which commissioned the familiar 8-ball version.

Mattel later bought rights to the product and gave it the name Magic 8 Ball. Inside each toy is an icosahedral (twenty-sided . . . duh!) die. Each facet of the die contains a probable answer to a yes or no question. All you need to do the next time you face a major life decision is shake the 8-ball and follow its orders.

---

flipism, goylate, adamatism

1. **flipism (FLIP-ihz-uhm) (noun):** The practice of making all decisions based on flipping a coin. The term originated in a Donald Duck comic book.

2. **goylate (GOY-luht) (adj. or adv.):** To paint in the manner of Francisco Goya. The word also refers to resultant works. Goya is best known for introducing subversive, imaginative elements into his art, which we tend to associate with the twentieth century.

3. **adamatism (ADUH-me-tiz-uhm) (noun):** The practice of going around naked; a state of being naked. The "Adam" of the word's root was an early advocate of nudism before he ate the fruit of the Tree of Knowledge, grew ashamed, yadda yadda yadda.

The fake word is:

goylate

Goya (1746–1828) first attained success as a court painter, but a mysterious illness in the 1790s (possibly mental, possibly not) appeared to act as the catalyst for the artist to explore darker realms of his psyche. Goya's so-called Black Paintings, painted directly onto the walls of his house, were the culmination of these impulses.

The best known of these works is *Saturn Devouring His Son*. The disturbing painting shows the Greek titan Saturn chewing the head off one of his sons, the way a child chews the head off her chocolate Easter bunny. The mythological Saturn ate each of his children for fear that one of them would overthrow him. Saturn's wife, Rhea, hides the couple's sixth child. True to the prediction, this child, Zeus, overthrows his father.

Flipping Off

Flipism, or at least the term, really does originate in a Donald Duck comic book. Written by Carl Banks, 1953's "Flip Decision" introduces Donald to Professor Batty. Batty, clearly not an accredited scientist, persuades Donald to make all his major life decisions by flipping a coin. Zaniness and an arrest (driving the wrong way on a one-way street) ensue.

---

creen, karadagh, trouvaille

1. **creen (CREEN) (verb, noun):** To see ghosts and spirits; to capture ghosts and spirits on film or in photographs. Also, the name of the resultant images. One famous creen features the Brown Lady of Raynham Hall, creened in 1936.

2. **karadagh (CAR-uh-dah) (noun):** A Persian rug with bold design and vibrant colors. Karadaghs are similar to the Ardabil Carpet found in London's Victoria and Albert Museum and in the Los Angeles County Museum of Art. The carpets were found in a mosque in the Iranian city of Ardabil, where they were being destroyed by foot traffic.

3. **trouvaille (true-VEE) (noun):** A lucky find. The word's origin is from the Old French term "trouver," which means "to find." In 1980, Australian Kevin Hillier uncovered quite the trouvaille. Using a metal detector, he discovered a 61-pound gold nugget, barely a foot below the ground. To this day, the nugget, named the Hand of Faith because it is shaped somewhat like a praying hand, is on display in Las Vegas's Golden Nugget Casino. Hillier sold the nugget to the casino for a cool million.

The fake word is:

creen

There may not be a "creen," but there is a Brown Lady. Photographers from *Country Life* magazine were simply at Raynham Hall to take some "harmless" pictures of the Norfolk estate in Great Britain. In addition to photos of gardens and antiques, one photographer also captured a clearly human image descending a main staircase. No one visible to the naked eye was on the staircase when the photo was shot.

Although the identity of the Brown Lady is disputed, sightings of the ghost began being reported in 1835. Perhaps camera-shy, the Brown Lady has rarely been seen since being "creened" in 1936.

Tut Tut

One of the world's greatest trouvailles is the tomb of King Tutankhamen, or King Tut, by Howard Carter in 1922. Actually, the entrance to the tomb was discovered by Carter's anonymous water boy. Nonetheless, when Carter explored the site, he found the best preserved tomb of an ancient pharaoh discovered to date.

The site is famously—though erroneously—deemed an unlucky find by those who believe in the "Curse of King Tut." Supposedly, everyone involved in Carter's expedition met mysterious and horrible deaths soon after discovering the tomb. Most of these stories are urban legends.

sungar, bundesstaat, mophilate

1. **sungar (SUHN-gar) (noun):** A small breastwork built around a natural hollow and intended to shield only a few men. Except for the fact that it's not made of snow, a sungar bears a striking resemblance to the kind of "fort" you make during a snowball fight.

2. **bundesstaat (BUN-duh-shtaht) (noun):** A federation. A federation is a group of self-governing states that "answer" to a central government. Germany is a federation, for example. So is The United Federation of Planets (of *Star Trek* fame).

3. **mophilate (MAH-fuh-luht) (verb):** To make stamps featuring celebrities. The United States does not issue stamps of living people. Presidents can be immortalized a year after they die, but fans of celebrities, statesmen, and history makers must wait ten years.

The fake word is:
mophilate

Elvis Presley got people all shook up in 1992 when the U.S. Postal Service, for the first time, let the American public choose a likeness for one of its stamps. The choice was between a likeness of the young Elvis or a painting of the older, Las Vegas-era Elvis.

The vote wasn't even close. More than a million ballots made it back to the postal service, and 75 percent of Elvis enthusiasts chose Mark Stutzman's image of the young King, half-sneer in place, clutching a microphone like a lover's hand.

Make It So

The United Federation of Planets, shortened typically to "The Federation," consists of 150 member planets (as of 2373) spread across 8,000 light years of the Milky Way.

The Federation has existed as long as *Star Trek*. Vague mentions of the Federation occur from the show's first episodes, and it is featured prominently in 1967's "A Taste of Armageddon." Show creator Gene Roddenberry viewed the Federation as an idealized version of the United Nations. He figured it prominently because *Star Trek* portrayed a vision of a peaceful intergalactic future that contrasted with the unrest that characterized the 1960s.

---

tumulose, rabato, prastin

1. **tumulose** (TOO-muh-lohss) (adj.): Covered with small hills or mounds. A "tumulus" is a burial mound.

2. **rabato** (ruh-BAH-doh) (noun): A wide, lace-edged collar prominent in the seventeenth century. Not to be confused with "Mr. Roboto," star of Styx's 1983 album *Kilroy Was Here*.

3. **prastin** (PRA-stihn) (noun): "Watered-down" versions of violent fiction or film. The detective genre, for instance, often contains graphic violence and sex. Prastins have been created to remove these objectionable components of the genre.

The fake word is:
prastin

If you love detective fiction, then you may be a fan of so-called cozy mysteries. Cozy mysteries are the antithesis of the hardboiled detective fiction prominent in the 1930s and 1940s, which was made into so many great film noirs of that period.

Cozy mysteries minimize sex and violence in their plots, or they treat them for laughs. The term itself was coined in the late twentieth century, but cozy mysteries have existed far longer. Agatha Christie's Miss Marple series, for example, is cozy as . . . a tea cosy, and she's been around since 1926.

Domo Arigato, **Mr. Roboto**

If you are a Gen Xer, then you remember Styx's 1983 song, "Mr. Roboto." The song, with its electronically altered voices and catchy chorus, reached number three on the Billboard charts.

Essentially, the song—and the album from which it was culled—is the story of a dystopian world in which rock 'n' roll is being destroyed by the forces of righteousness who believe that "rock is bad, m'kay." These "good guys" try to turn music lovers into robots, but "Kilroy" bursts free of this awful place and makes it okay to rock.

---

flype, moffan, slavocracy

1. **flype (FLYPE) (verb):** To strip off, as a stocking; to peel, as a fruit. In 1976, New York's Kathy Wafler Madison, just sixteen, set a record for the world's longest apple peel. She managed to flype an apple with such finesse that she left a peel 172 feet, four inches long.

2. **moffan (MAH-fihn) (noun):** Necklace characterized by small shells strung on a leather cord. Heartthrobs of the 1970s wore these, and they've made a comeback in recent years.

3. **slavocracy (slay-VOCK-ruh-see) (noun):** A powerful Antebellum faction of slave owners and slavery advocates. Many members of this class referred to themselves instead as a "plantocracy" because they belonged to the planter class. Apparently, they found the name "slavocracy"—but not the practice of owning slaves—distasteful.

The fake word is:

moffan

A moffan is better known as a puka-shell necklace. If there were a puka-shell necklace hall of fame—and a quick search of the term indicates there isn't—one man surely would be its main event: David Cassidy. The teen idol made guys wearing necklaces cool. Prior to Cassidy, most dudes wouldn't be caught dead with jewelry around their necks.

"Puka," by the way, is the Hawaiian word for "hole," and it refers to the fact that puka shells have naturally occurring holes, which made them perfect for stringing onto a necklace or bracelet. In the wild, the shells, many of which are now man-made, are cone snail shells. In Hawaiian lore, wearing puka shells is supposed to guarantee one a safe and peaceful voyage.

Profile in Courage

Southern abolitionist?!? These two words don't go together, do they? Not often, but they do if one is discussing Virginia's Moncure Conway.

Conway's family owned slaves, and his father and brothers remained pro-slavery all their lives. Conway, never avidly pro-slavery, became completely anti-slavery after becoming familiar with Ralph Waldo Emerson's transcendentalist philosophy. If the "soul" transcends all bonds of earthly judgment, then how can anyone rightfully be "owned" by anyone else?

Conway was educated in New England and returned to Virginia. Before long, his abolitionist views and efforts on behalf of a runaway slave made life in Dixie dangerous. Conway moved about the country before ultimately settling (and later dying) in France.

---

elantish, glumpish, adpromissor

1. **elantish** (uh-LAHN-tish) (adj.): Given to or characterized by involvement in a segregated social group. If you belonged to a clique in high school, then you demonstrated elantish behavior.

2. **glumpish** (GLUHM-pish) (adj.): Somewhat grumpy. *Mr. Grumpy* is the name of the twenty-seventh book in British author Roger Hargreaves's popular "Mr. Men" series.

3. **adpromissor** (ad-PRO-mizz-uhr) (noun): A "lawyer word" for "bail." Duane Chapman, a.k.a. "Dog the Bounty Hunter" has done more than anyone on earth to make adpromissor cool.

The fake word is:

elantish

Despite the continued success of John Hughes's *The Breakfast Club*, high schools are not limited to just five cliques.

- Burnouts. These (usually) guys are always either fully baked or half-baked on booze, marijuana, Liquid Paper, or God only knows what else.
- Art Geeks. These folks belong to the chorus, art club, AV club, drama club, etc.
- Out of Your Leagues. These girls would never, ever talk to you unless you were a . . .
- Big Men on Campus. These guys, usually jocks, get all the great girls. They spend a good portion of their life reliving their "glory days."
- Dorks/Dweebs. They get pooped on in school, but someday will run the world, and they know it.
- God Squad. These kids are "saving themselves" for marriage, and name-drop Jesus regularly.
- Squares. These kids go to school to LEARN. How dorky is that?
- Goths/Emos. Life is SO HARD for these pampered suburban kids.

Just Call Him Dog

No one rocks a mullet and sunglasses quite like Duane "Dog" Chapman, the man who has made many kids consider a future that entails chasing after people who have skipped bail.

Since 2004, Dog has brought his patented mix of profanity and spiritual awareness to A&E's *Dog the Bounty Hunter*. (He isn't always one of the good guys.)

loutrophoros, spaltice, hounce

1. **loutrophoros (loo-TRAHPH-uh-ruhss) (noun):** A tall, long-necked ceremonial vase used in ancient Greece. Used to hold water during marriages and funerals, these were placed into the tombs of the unmarried.

2. **spaltice (SPAHL-tiss) (noun):** A hair-styling tool. These are used primarily to help people achieve the "mullet," which is a combination of short hair and long hair. Affectionately referred to as "business in the front, party in the back."

3. **hounce (HOWNTZ) (noun):** An ornament on a cart horse's collar. If you're putting the cart before the horse, do you put the hounce before the horse too? The mind reels.

The fake word is:

spaltice

The mullet, as most are aware, is a hairstyle that features short bangs and sides accompanied by hair growing as far down one's back as one can make it grow. The style first gained prominence in the 1970s. David Bowie's Ziggy Stardust rocked a mullet, and so did Wings-era Paul McCartney. The 1980s brought us such mullet-sporters as Michael Bolton, Phil Collins, and Anthony Geary ("Luke" of *General Hospital* fame).

Then along came Hannah Montana's dad. To this day, say "mullet," and people picture Billy Ray Cyrus, who owned the pop and country charts in 1992 with "Achy Breaky Heart." The song was a number one hit, and so was Cyrus's mullet, poised as it was above chiseled features and "guns" (biceps) visible thanks to denim jackets with torn-off sleeves.

On the Side, Clyde

The days of cart horses are mostly past, but one team still holds sway over the popular imagination: the Budweiser Clydesdales.

The Clydesdales, still used in commercials and for promotional activities to this day, first appeared in 1933. They celebrated the repeal of Prohibition. This original team of Clydesdales carried the first legal batch of Budweiser through the streets of St. Louis, Budweiser's home. Budweiser patriarch August Busch Sr. knew a good gimmick when he saw one. He sent another team of Clydesdales to the White House, so it could personally deliver beer to FDR.

lictic, untimeous, vaishnavism

1. **lictic (LICK-tick) (adj.):** Infested with lice. "Lice" is an umbrella term, encompassing more than 3,000 species of wingless insects that belong to the Phthiraptera order.

2. **untimeous (uhn-TIHM-ee-uhss) (adj.):** Untimely. Hollywood and popular music, unfortunately, are rife with untimeous deaths.

3. **vaishnavism (VISH-nuh-vihz-uhm) (noun):** The worship of Vishnu. Vishnu, according to believers, is one of the five primary forms of God. The others are Shiva, Devi, Surya, and Ganesha.

The fake word is:

lictic

Eww, you've got cooties! If you heard this on the playground, then you've been talking to a member of the opposite sex. All little girls know that boys are a hotbed of cooties, and all little boys know that just talking to a girl can infest you with an incurable case of this dread disease.

You may not know that "cooties" actually exist, and no, I'm not just talking about the children's game with the cute plastic "bugs." For the Doughboys of WWI, "cooties" were lice. The term appears in a 1917 service dictionary and in memoirs of World War I soldiers.

Most likely, the word "cooties" is derived from the word "kutu," which means lice. "Kutu" can be found in several languages of the Pacific region.

The Life You Save

Still worshipped by disaffected teens everywhere, James Byron Dean is one of Hollywood's most culturally resonant untimely deaths. The twenty-four-year-old was killed in 1955, just before his best-known film, *Rebel Without a Cause*, was released. Perhaps it was the combination of his moody good looks, the film's sad and passionate story, and the knowledge that Dean was dead that made him the quintessential "live fast, die young, leave a good-looking corpse" icon.

Ironically, just before his death from a car crash, Dean filmed a public service spot urging people to drive safely. The final line of the spot was, "Drive careful 'cuz the life you save might be mine."

---

dompt, knaur, olptic

1. **dompt (DAHMPT) (verb):** To hold a lion at bay. One early lion tamer was George Wombwell. During the Victorian era, Wombwell toured with Wombwell's Travelling Menagerie. He also is the man credited with the saying, "What can you give a man who has everything?"

2. **knaur (NO-uhr) (noun):** A knot on a piece of wood. In 2010, a New Haven, Connecticut, man discovered a knot on one of his trees that resembled Jesus Christ. (Or maybe Che Guevara. Or maybe any guy with a beard.)

3. **olptic (OHLPT-ick) (adj.):** Of or related to a romance begun at sea. For nearly a decade, people made olptic connections on the Pacific Princess, better known to TV viewers as *The Love Boat*.

The fake word is:

olptic

One of *The Love Boat's* oddest guests was pop artist Andy Warhol, who appeared in a 1985 episode.

Warhol wasn't looking for love. Instead, he played himself. The plot involving him pivoted around a chance meeting with one of his old "superstars." Warhol called the actors who worked on his experimental, often erotically charged films "superstars."

The "superstar" didn't want her flamboyant past to sink her new love affair with a straitlaced man. Warhol doesn't say much in the episode, but in his diary, he writes repeatedly about how nervous he is about just saying the line, "Hi, Mary."

By the way . . . the "superstar" is played by, of all people, Marion Ross, better known as Richie Cunningham's mom on *Happy Days* (!).

The Face of God

Jesus isn't just found on trees. He really seems to have a jones for food and food-related items.

- In 1978, a New Mexican woman found that the burn marks on her tortilla bore a striking resemblance to Christ.
- In 2006, a Texan found that random scraping in his frying pan had produced the visage of Christ.
- Jesus's mom has gotten into the action as well. Floridian Diana Duyser made a grilled cheese in 1994. After she took her first bite, she was amazed to see that burn marks on the toast bore an uncanny resemblance to the Virgin Mary. Duyser kept the toast on her nightstand for a decade and then sold it online in 2004. The winning bidder, an online casino, spent $28,000 (!) for the Virgin Mary Grilled Cheese.

hylochoric, remuda, williwaw

1. **hylochoric (HIGH-low-core-ick) (adj.):** Of or related to obesity-causing foods. Americans spend more than $6 billion on potato chips each year.

2. **remuda (ruh-MOOD-uh) (noun):** The herd of saddle horses from which ranch hands choose for a day's work. The word comes from the Spanish meaning "change of horses."

3. **williwaw (WILL-ee-waw) (noun):** Violent commotion or agitation; a sudden storm. Americans say "tempest in a teapot." Brits say "storm in a teacup."

The fake word is:
hylochoric

Saratoga Springs, New York. 1853. Chef George Crum is probably used to people complaining about the food in his elegant resort. What are you gonna do? But one guy keeps sending back his steak fries, claiming they're too thick.

Crum decides he'll show this dude a thin fry. He cuts the potatoes so thin that they can't possibly be picked up with a fork (the preferred method for fry-eating in those days). Crum sends out his order and waits for the fireworks. He gets them, but they're not what he expected. The guest is thrilled by these "potato chips."

Before long, people come to Saratoga Springs just to get some for themselves. Consequently, another early name for potato chips is "Saratoga chips."

Chill Out

To make a "tempest in a teapot" or "storm in a teacup" is to make a really big deal about something that's not too important. Perhaps we human beings tend to make mountains out of molehills (to steal another, similar phrase) because we feel increasingly out of control of the things in our lives that truly matter.

The American phrase for freaking out over nothing dates back to an 1838 editorial in *The United States Democratic Review*. It was used to describe the furor over a Supreme Court decision. The British phrase is even older, by some three hundred years. And both Brits and Yanks were beaten to the punch by Cicero's Latin phrase, which translated means "He was stirring up waves in a ladle."

---

xylary, bimelerite, myerst

1. **xylary (ZIGH-luh-ree) (adj.):** Related to, associated with, or composed of wood. Thanks to ventriloquism, many people believe that wood has a personality.

2. **bimelerite (BIME-luh-rite) (noun, usually capitalized):** Another term for a Zoarite. The Zoarites were a nineteenth-century separatist society that flourished briefly in Ohio.

3. **myerst (ME-urst) (verb):** To tinker. The Tinkertoy Construction Set debuted in 1913, and it has been creating stuff that gets caught in the vacuum cleaner ever since. The word comes from the Norwegian word *emyerst*, meaning "to fiddle with" or "to adjust."

The fake word is:

myerst

The Erector Set came first. It was invented in 1911 by A. C. Gilbert. Children could tinker with metal beams, nuts, bolts, and even electric motors. In 1949, an Erector Set was used to create a model of the first artificial heart. Many years later, ironically, Dr. Jack Kevorkian used an Erector Set to create a model of his assisted suicide machine (!).

Charles H. Pajeau and Robert Pettit of Evanston, Illinois, created Tinkertoys in 1913. Pajeau was inspired after watching children play with pencils and empty spools of thread. These simple bits of wood and plastic have been used since then to create objects as complex as Ferris wheels, robots, and even a tic-tac-toe-playing computer.

The Fine Art of Gastromancy

Nowadays, "ventriloquism" calls to mind wiseass blocks of wood with human features who let fly a string of stinging comebacks for the enjoyment of an audience. Once upon a time, however, ventriloquism was a sacred art.

The ancient Greeks called ventriloquism "gastromancy," which basically means "from the stomach." The voices some appeared able to "throw" were believed to originate in the stomach of the speaker. They were thought to be the voices of the dead. As a result, gastromancers were revered because they could "interepret" these voices and use them to foretell the future.

By the nineteenth century, most people realized that ventriloquism was just a parlor trick and it lost its spiritual origins. The word "ventriloquism," by the way, comes from the Latin words "venter" (belly) and "loqui" (speak). Romans also believed the voices emerged from people's bellies.

nerf, dossennus, lynge

1. **nerf (NUHRF) (verb):** No, it's not the spongy ball. It's to bump into another car during an automobile race. The worst racing disaster in history occurred in 1955 at Le Mans, and it was due to nerfing.

2. **dossennus (duh-SENN-us) (noun):** A sharp-witted hunchback that is a stock character in Roman comedies. Quasimodo, the "star" of Victor Hugo's *The Hunchback of Notre Dame,* is a remnant of this stock character.

3. **lynge (LINJH) (verb):** To cry incessantly, especially in an overly dramatic fashion. In 1951, Johnnie Ray and The Four Lads released "Cry," which went on to top both the pop and R&B charts. Ray is best remembered for his overly dramatic performances, both on vinyl and in concert. He could lynge like nobody's business.

The fake word is:

lynge

Ray's song, penned by Churchill Kohlman, isn't the only hit simply called "Cry."

- Godley & Crème's song reached number sixteen on the Billboard charts in 1985.
- Faith Hill's song, written by Angie Aparo, hit number one on the adult contemporary chart in 2002 and stayed at that position for an amazing eleven weeks.
- Mandy Moore's "Cry" never hit the charts in the United States, but it was a hit in Canada and in many Asian countries.
- British artist Kym Marsh's song went to number two on the U.K. singles chart in 2003.
- And an honorary mention must go to the great Johnny Cash. Not content with just one "cry," Cash recorded the song "Cry! Cry! Cry!" in 1955, just as his career was heating up.

Disaster at Le Mans

During the third hour of the 24 Hours of Le Mans race in 1955, driver Pierre Levegh clipped Lance Macklin's Austin-Healey and was forced to make an evasive move. Levegh hit an earthen bank, and his Mercedes-Benz 300 SLR flew into the air.

As it flew, it disintegrated, showering the crowd in flaming debris. Levegh was killed after being thrown from the car. The flames and debris killed eighty-two spectators and injured one hundred more. Despite the horrific accident, the race continued. Organizers feared a mass exodus for the gates would have prevented the timely arrival of emergency vehicles.

---

oecus, brundle, duddie

1. **oecus (EEK-us) (noun):** A room or living quarters in an ancient Roman house. Sometimes, the oecus was used as a triclinium, or formal dining room.

2. **brundle (BRUHN-dl) (verb):** To carry a load. The songwriting team of Bobby Scott and Bob Russell wrote "He Ain't Heavy, He's My Brother" in 1969. The song, of course, is about brundling someone who needs help getting through life. A British Invasion band, The Hollies, released a recording of the song that year—featuring Elton John on piano—which reached the top ten in both American and the U.K.

3. **duddie (DUH-dee) (adj.):** Ragged, tattered. This can refer to, say, a flag left out in the rain and wind, or to someone who's been working so hard that he or she feels just duddie . . . the opposite of "just duckie."

The fake word is:

brundle

The late 1960s were a weighty time, no doubt. Perhaps that's why, in addition to the song made popular by The Hollies, two other popular groups of the day had brundly songs of their own.

The Band, which had supported Bob Dylan before going solo, released its debut album *Music from Big Pink* in 1968. One of the platter's best-known songs is called "The Weight." Although the tune didn't make it into the American top forty, it is well known because of its use in films and its presence on "classic rock" stations.

The same year the Hollies recorded "He Ain't Heavy," The Beatles released their last album, *Abbey Road* (*Let It Be* was released later but recorded earlier.) Side two of the record features a couple of medleys, one of which includes the song "Carry That Weight." Written by Paul McCartney, the song makes oblique references to the business and personal squabbles that would soon break up the band.

Just Duckie

Before he played Charlie Sheen's sane brother on *Two and a Half Men*, Jon Cryer was probably best known as the luckless Phil "Duckie" Dale from 1986's *Pretty in Pink*. In the film, Duckie is obsessed with Andie Walsh, for whom Duckie is just a friend. Andie is herself obsessed with a guy named Blane (!). The original version of the film follows Andie's trials and tribulations and ends with her realizing that Duckie is a better fit than Blane.

Test audiences *hated* this conclusion, and the filmmakers re-shot it. This time, Andie chooses Blane and Duckie bows out gracefully. Many viewers since have disagreed strongly with the assessment of that original test audience.

fronch, blinter, craton

1. **fronch** (FRAHNCH) (verb): To tickle with a feather. "Tickle" is from the Middle English "tikelen," which means "to touch lightly." Tickling may seem insignificant, but some of the greatest minds in history have given philosophical glances to the phenomenon. Among them are Plato, Francis Bacon, Galileo, and Charles Darwin.

2. **blinter** (BLIHN-tuhr) (verb): To flicker or glimmer; to blink. The best known version of "The Glow-Worm" was recorded by the Mills Brothers in 1952. It spent three weeks at number one.

3. **craton** (KRAY-tuhn) (noun): A stable and reasonably immobile mass that serves as the "base" of a continent or the basin of an ocean. Some craton examples are Canada's Slave craton, the United States' Wyoming craton, and South America's Amazonian craton.

The fake word is:
fronch

Here are some ticklish facts.

- There are two types of tickling. The light kind, which typically doesn't induce laughter, is called knismesis. The heavier, laughter-inducing type is called gargalesis.
- Tickle torture was a popular form of punishment for Chinese nobility during the Han Dynasty (206 B.C. to A.D. 220).
- The Romans also used this form of torture. Victims would have their feet dipped in a salt solution. A goat would then come to lick off the solution.
- MRI experiments show that we can't tickle ourselves because our brain reacts differently to tickling from ourselves than it does to tickling from others.
- Galileo used tickling as a metaphor for our perception of reality.

Shine Little Glow-Worm, Glimmer

The Mills Brothers weren't the first to record "The Glow-Worm." Their version had lyrics that had been re-worked by the immortal Johnny Mercer. Prior to Mercer, the song was first translated into English by Lilla Cayley Robinson and used in a 1920 Broadway musical, *The Girl Behind the Counter*.

The song first blintered to life in 1902, and it was originally entitled "Das Gluhwurmchen" ("The Glow-Worm"). The song was written as an aria and performed in Paul Lincke's mini-opera, *Lysistrata*.

tomple, injucundity, canader

1. **tomple** (TAHM-pull) (noun): A ceremonial bowl used by tribes indigenous to America's West Coast. Early Spanish explorers mention "tomples" in several of their journals.

2. **injucundity** (in-joo-KUHN-dih-tee) (noun): Unpleasantness. It shares a root with the word "jocund," which means "cheerful" or "merry."

3. **canader** (KAHN-uh-duhr) (noun): A canoe. The term is principally used in Britain. This is ironic, of course, because canoes trace their history to the indigenous peoples of North America.

The fake word is:
tomple

California wouldn't be California without Fray (Father) Junipero Serra (1713–1784).

He had a zeal for mission work that included such odd tactics as pounding himself on the chest with a rock while preaching. At other times, he would whip himself, and once or twice he applied a lit torch to his chest.

Despite (or perhaps because of?) these unorthodox methods, the Spanish government made Serra head of a group of Franciscan monks charged with creating missions in what is today California. In all, Serra established twenty-one missions (twenty-two if you count one in Baja).

But Serra's reputation has suffered over the years. He beat and otherwise mistreated many of the Native Americans he was supposed to be serving. If tomples existed, Serra would likely have destroyed them, as he did many aspects of indigenous culture. Despite this, Pope John Paul II beatified Serra in 1988.

Jocund Injucundity

Apparently, people require—nay, demand—a relatively stable mix of joy and misery. The term "hedonic treadmill" has been coined to describe this urge.

Regardless of most major negative or positive events that occur in one's life, one ultimately will seek a level of happiness that is familiar. For example, let's say you win the lottery. Great! Once you've got that money, though, you will have new expectations, change your lifestyle, and acquire new issues. The end result is that you will be left at the same level of happiness you had before getting that windfall. In effect, you're on a treadmill, always trying to maintain a constant speed. The term originated in a 1971 essay entitled "Hedonic Relativism and Planning the Good Society."

---

grobianism, mebos, interlatinous

1. **grobianism (GROW-bee-uhn-ihz-uhm) (noun, usually capitalized):** Boorish behavior. The word derives from St. Grobian, the fictional patron saint of coarse and rude people.

2. **mebos (ME-bus) (noun):** A dessert made from salted and sugared dried apricots that's especially popular in South Africa.

3. **interlatinous (ihn-tuhr-LAHT-uh-nuhss) (adj.):** Of or related to any of a family of languages that began evolving from Latin but never attained enough derivation to become new languages. Linguists estimate that the world has between three thousand and five thousand interlatinous languages.

The fake word is:
interlatinous

The "facts" about interlatinous languages are a complete fabrication, but linguists do argue over how many unique Romance Languages—those that "began life" as Latin—exist. The approximate number of Romance Languages is twenty-five, but don't tell people who speak different dialects of dominant languages that they aren't unique. The most common Romance Languages are Spanish, Italian, Portuguese, French, Romanian, and Catalan.

These languages actually don't derive from "Latin" per se. They derive from so-called "vulgar Latin," the language used in Rome by the Roman equivalent of "just plain folks." The hoity-toity wrote and spoke in classical Latin, but merchants, soldiers, etc., spoke in vulgar Latin. The term "Romance Language" derives from the fact that these languages descend from "Roman" speech, not "Latin" speech.

You're Such a Grobian!

St. Grobian makes his first appearance in Alsatian satirist Sebastian Brant's *Das Narrenschiff*, better known to us as *Ship of Fools*. *Ship of Fools* first appeared in 1494, and it was immediately popular. The mock epic focuses on what Brant viewed as the excesses of the Roman Catholic Church. It was immensely popular and translated into numerous languages. Although Brant himself did not support the Protestant Reformation, many of the excesses satirized in his book were the very ones targeted by Reformers.

Nearly four hundred years after Brant's work first appeared, Katherine Anne Porter borrowed his title for her own *Ship of Fools*. The 1962 novel focuses on passengers sailing from Mexico to Europe aboard a German freighter. Porter's work is an allegory on the rise of Nazism.

---

anticreeper, dontrello, isthmian

1. **anticreeper** (AN-tie-cree-puhr) (noun): A device that keeps railroad tracks from moving. Unfortunately, anticreepers would not have done anything to stop a 1910 train disaster in Wellington, Washington, that killed ninety-six people. An avalanche swooped down on two trains that were forced to stop near the town due to wintry conditions.

2. **dontrello** (dahn-TRELL-oh) (noun): A buffoonish stock character in opera. Mozart was fond of using dontrellos in his popular operas.

3. **isthmian** (IHZ-me-uhn) (noun): One who lives on an isthmus. The most important isthmus in the world, arguably, is the Isthmus of Panama.

The fake word is:
dontrello

He may not have lived to be forty years old, but Wolfgang Amadeus Mozart was a very prolific composer. One reason he was able to produce so much during his short lifetime is because he got a head start. The precocious Mozart was an accomplished violinist by age five, and he started composing before his teens.

His earliest opera, for example, was composed when Mozart was just eleven. *Die Schuldigkeit des ersten Gebots* (*The Obligation of the First and Foremost Commandment*) is a sacred drama with a libretto credited to "J.A.W." Scholars today believe J.A.W. is Ignaz Anton von Weiser.

Mozart actually only composed the first part of the opera, but the other two parts have disappeared. Mozart's section premiered on March 12, 1767, in Salzburg's Knight's Hall of the Palace of the Archbishop.

It Ain't Just an Isthmus

The Isthmus of Panama may be home to the eponymous country and to the Panama Canal, but it doesn't have a lock on "Panama."

- Van Halen released the single "Panama" in 1984.
- Panama hats actually originate in Ecuador. From there, they are shipped to the Isthmus of Panama and on to spots all over the globe. Hence, Panama gets credit for these popular summer accoutrements.
- The following states have a Panama: California, Illinois, Iowa, Nebraska, and Oklahoma. Florida has a Panama City and a Panama City Beach.
- Sri Lanka has a Panama Beach.

badchen, gony, wastrelism

1. **badchen (BAHT-kuhn) (noun):** A professional jester at Jewish wedding celebrations. Some particularly fancy weddings might also include a *letz* (musician) and a *marshalik* (master of ceremonies).

2. **gony (GO-nee) (noun):** An idiot; one who acts gooney or like an idiot. The children in the popular 1985 film *The Goonies* are so named because they come from the "Goon Docks" region of Astoria, Oregon.

3. **wastrelism (WASE-truh-lihz-uhm) (noun):** A philosophical approach to profligacy. The term was coined and became popular following the release of the 1998 cult film *The Big Lebowski*.

The fake word is:
wastrelism

Despite the fact that "wastrelism" isn't a real word, Jeffrey "The Dude" Lebowski has indeed made being wastrel into a pseudoscience—or at least into an art form.

In the Coen brothers' film, Lebowski gets mistaken for another, wealthy Jeffrey Lebowski. Zaniness ensues—but through it all, Lebowski manages to stay fairly calm. Of course, liberal doses of marijuana and White Russians help. On the rare occasions when The Dude does lose his cool, his best buddy decries him for being "very un-dude."

Allusions to The Dude's intellect and past as a campus radical pepper the film, which is why he has become a cult saint. He chooses a profligate lifestyle and somehow manages to make it work for himself. As Lebowski himself says, "The Dude abides."

Curse of the Coreys

The Goonies of *The Goonies* are poor kids who get involved in outlandish freebooting (piracy) adventures in order to save their neighborhood. The film features an early Corey Feldman. Feldman, along with fellow actor Corey Haim, were known as "the two Coreys" because they were actors that shared the same first name. Both were huge stars in the 1980s whose careers took a downturn afterward.

Feldman managed to overcome addiction and early success and has become a denizen of reality television and minor films. Haim, unfortunately, wasn't as lucky. He fell into drug addiction but appeared to overcome it in the early 2000s, and began to star with Feldman on a reality show called *The Two Coreys*. But Haim began to backslide and died of a suspected overdose in 2010.

treemic, usquebaugh, dispark

1. **treemic (TREE-mick) (adj.):** Predisposed to bleeding disorders. The formal name for most bleeding disorders is coagulopathy. Coagulation is blood-clotting. If a person's blood clots too slowly, that's called hypocoagulability, and if it clots too slowly, that's called hypercoagulability. And if you're losing blood for no discernible reason, a vampire may be to blame.

2. **usquebaugh (US-kwuh-bah) (noun):** Whiskey; or, a type of spicy cordial. In Gaelic, "usquebaugh" means "water of life."

3. **dispark (DISS-park) (verb):** To open to the public a previously private park. Since Michael Jackson began proceedings to sell it, and especially since his death, speculation has been rampant that the King of Pop's private amusement park—Neverland Ranch—will open to the public.

The fake word is:

treemic

Before the popularity of the *Twilight* series, if one said "vampire" only one face would come to mind: Bela Lugosi's. For Lugosi himself, that was both a blessing and a curse. Look up the word "typecast" and you might well see a picture of the Hungarian actor in his trademark cape sporting his widow's peak hairstyle.

Lugosi began his acting career in his native Hungary before emigrating to the United States and becoming a naturalized citizen. His first American film role was a part in 1923's *The Silent Command.* At this point, Lugosi was known principally as a romantic leading man (no one could hear his accent in silent films).

Lugosi first appeared as Dracula on Broadway in 1927. Two years later, he was picked for the lead in Universal Studio's 1931 film version of the play. From that point forward, Lugosi was typecast as a villain or horror film actor, and he wasn't keen on this. Nonetheless, some sixty years after his death, many still know the name "Bela Lugosi."

Peter Pan in California

Michael Jackson purchased the land that would become the Neverland Valley Ranch in 1988. Over the years, Jackson turned part of the property into an amusement park—he put in two trains, a Ferris wheel, a carousel, a roller coaster, and bumper cars. Periodically, he would open the park to area children.

After allegations of sexual misconduct with a minor were leveled against the singer, Jackson began to distance himself from Neverland. Foreclosure proceedings on the property began in 2007, and Jackson sold it in 2008, a year before his death.

exultet, recreant, polotkus

1. **exultet (ig-ZOOL-tet) (noun):** An Easter eve hymn of praise sung in the Roman Catholic Church. The word is also spelled exsultet. An exsultet is sung following a procession with the Paschal candle, a large white candle blessed and lit at Easter.

2. **recreant (REH-kree-uhnt) (adj.):** Describes someone crying for mercy in the heat of battle. He never exactly gets his "red badge of courage," but Henry Fleming, protagonist of *The Red Badge of Courage*, never cries for mercy in the heat of battle, either.

3. **polotkus (puh-LOT-kuss) (noun):** A type of indoor football popular in the Midwest. The Midwest—possibly Ohio, possibly Michigan—also gave us the bean bag-tossing game cornhole. Players take turns tossing bean bags toward—and hopefully through—a round hole cut into a sloping board.

The fake word is:
polotkus

If you've ever played table football, better known in the United States as foosball, you've probably wondered what a "foos" is. The word "foosball" is a corruption of the German word "fussball" (pronounced like "foosball"), which means "foot ball," the name everyone outside of America calls soccer.

Evan Dube invented the first modern version of foosball in 1921. He loved soccer and wanted to create a version of it that could be played inside the home. His uncle, who lived in the United States, saw his nephew's invention and patented his own version of the game in 1927.

So Little Time

The greatest novel about the U.S. Civil War was written by a man not born until six years after Appomattox. Stephen Crane wrote *The Red Badge of Courage* in 1895 while only in his mid-20s. Although the novel does not mention a specific battle, most academics believe the novel focuses on Chancellorsville. Crane achieved realism by interviewing elderly Civil War veterans and by reading contemporary accounts of battles.

Despite dying of tuberculosis at only twenty-eight, Crane also was a master of the short story form and a pioneer in the literary traditions of realism and naturalism. At his death, Crane was largely forgotten, but it didn't take long before he took his rightful place as one of America's most innovative writers.

---

haikai, plupose, Weissnichtwo

1. **haikai (HIGH-KIGH) (noun):** Playful Japanese verse, popular during the later feudal ages. Yes, it sounds similar to the more familiar "haiku," but it is a different form. Haiku tends to focus on nature and usually has a jarring twist or observation at its conclusion. Haikai is akin to straightforward lyric poetry, and one of its greatest practitioners was Basho (1644–1694).

2. **plupose (PLOO-pohss) (adj.):** Of or related to animals with pouches used for carrying young. Marsupials are plupose animals, and similar animals include opossums, kangaroos, wombats, anteaters, Tasmanian devils, and koalas.

3. **Weissnichtwo (VI-snick-voh) (noun, usually capitalized):** An imaginary, unknown, or indefinite place. The word is German for "know not where," and Weissnichtwo first appears in Thomas Carlyle's *Sartor Resartus* ("The Tailor Re-tailored").

The fake word is:
plupose

Most people only know of the carnivorous marsupial, the Tasmanian devil, because of Warner Brothers's Looney Tunes.

The Tazmanian Devil, also known as Taz, is the "youngest" Looney Tunes character, whose older "brothers" include Bugs Bunny, Daffy Duck, and Porky Pig. He first appeared in 1954's "Devil May Hare," in which he terrorizes Bugs, who avoids being eaten due to his usual craftiness.

Only five cartoons featuring Taz were made prior to Warner Brothers shutting down its animation studio in 1964. Nonetheless, he has remained a popular character and was "drawn into" new adventures in the 1990s.

Poioumena (?!?)

Carlyle's *Sartor Resartus*, which contains Weissnichtwo, is "post-modern" even though it appeared nearly a century before modern-ism. Nonetheless, it is a type of fiction called poioumena, which describes metafiction about the process of creation. Metafiction is fiction that always reminds the reader that it's fiction. It is not intended to create verisimilitude. Got all that?

Carlyle's work, therefore, is classed with the even older (and somewhat better known) *Tristram Shandy* by Laurence Sterne, as well as with "true" postmodern works such as Vladimir Nabo-kov's *Pale Fire* and Salman Rushdie's *Midnight's Children*.

---

pommettee, revirescent, plascent

1. **pommettee (PAH-mah-tay) (adj.):** Describes ornamentation on a cross that resembles small balls or circles. The cross shape has attracted human beings since they began walking around upright. Some carvings in Stone Age-era European caves are in the cross shape. They did not, however, feature pommettees.

2. **revirescent (REHV-uh-rehss-uhnt) (adj.):** Growing young or fresh again; reviving. The concept of a "Fountain of Youth," a mystical spring that can reverse the aging process, appeared as early as the writings of Herodotus. Herodotus, who lived from 484 B.C. to 425 B.C., is known as the "Father of History."

3. **plascent (PLACE-uhnt) (adj.):** Pleasant or pleasing to the ear. According to those who study phonoaesthetics (the "science" of pleasing and displeasing sounds), the words "cellar door" are the most plascent in the English language.

The fake word is:

plascent

The word is fake, but the "cellar door" assertion is true. It has been made by many.

- William Dean Howells, journalist and author of the realist novel *The Rise of Silas Lapham*, discusses the euphonious quality of "cellar door" in a 1905 article that appeared in *Harper's* magazine.

- Some academics have argued that Edgar Allen Poe's famous poem "The Raven" owes something to "cellar door." Poe, these academics claim, loved the beauty of this phrase and approximated it in "The Raven" by using the recurring phrase "nevermore."

- And even though he wasn't the first to claim that "cellar door" is the most pleasant (though essentially meaningless) set of words in the English language, the claim is nonetheless often attributed to J. R. R. Tolkien. The author of *The Lord of the Rings* discussed "cellar door" in his 1955 essay "English and Welsh."

The Fountain of Youth

Ponce de Leon, the Spanish explorer who "discovered" Florida, was really trying to find the fabled Fountain of Youth when he landed in present-day St. Augustine in 1513.

At least that's what tourism officials would like for you to believe.

In fact, there's no evidence that de Leon ever looked for the Fountain of Youth, and there's certainly no evidence that he claimed to find it. Most "evidence" presented is based on the historical accounts of people who had an axe to grind with the explorer. Gonzalo Fernandez de Oviedo's *Historia General y Natural de las Indias* (1535), for example, suggests that de Leon was looking for the Fountain of Youth in order to cure his impotence (!).

capuan, blunster, slinge

1. **Capuan (CAP-yuh-wuhn) (adj., usually capitalized):** Luxurious. The word derives from Capua, an ancient Roman city renowned for its luxury.

2. **blunster (BLUNTS-tuhr) (verb):** To brag about nonexistent accomplishments. Every boy who has ever been in a locker room has engaged in blunstering about his nonexistent sexual escapades.

3. **slinge (SLINJH) (verb):** To loaf or hang around somewhere. Some European countries use a device called The Mosquito to discourage loitering youths. The device emits frequencies that typically can only be heard by young people, since the ability to hear higher frequencies decreases with age. Opponents of the device fear it violates young people's civil rights and may even cause hearing damage.

The fake word is:
blunster

But the world is full of braggarts. Many people have had something to say about them.

- "Heroes are not known by the loftiness of their carriage; the greatest braggarts are generally the greatest cowards." –Jean-Jacques Rousseau
- "Who knows himself a braggart, / Let him fear this, for it will come to pass / That every braggart shall be found an ass." –William Shakespeare
- "Mules are always boasting that their ancestors were horses." –German proverb
- "When boasting ends, there dignity begins." –Owen Young (General Electric chairman)
- "It's a weak nation, like a weak person, that must behave with bluster and boasting and rashness and other signs of insecurity." –Jimmy Carter

---

Poverty Sucks

If you've got the ability to sneer at poverty, then you may consider some of the following capuan resorts. The Penthouse Suite at Canne's Martinez Hotel will set you back a cool $18,000 a night. Amenities include a private butler on call twenty-four hours a day. The Royal Suite at Dubai's Burj al Arab will set you back $19,000 per night, but you do get a rotating four-poster bed. If you've got $34,000 to burn, then you can get a night in the Ty Warner Penthouse of New York's famed Four Seasons Hotel in which you get your own waterfall and grand piano. And you can get a taste of the Playboy life for just $40,000 a night. That will get you a stay in the Hugh Hefner Sky Villa of Las Vegas's Palm Casino. (Playboy Bunnies not included.)

torkmeat, bellicist, silentious

1. **torkmeat (TORK-MEAT) (noun):** Military speak for leg wounds. Every war gives us colorful new words invented by service personnel. The Iraq War, for example, has given us expressions such as "embrace the suck" (basically, "just deal with it whatever it is") and words like "fobbits," a derogatory term for soldiers who rarely leave protected areas (called FOBs, or "Forward Operations Base")

2. **bellicist (BELL-uh-sist) (noun):** One who advocates war. Sometimes, if there isn't a pressing need for it, countries including the United States have "invented" reasons urging the country into war. For example, the Spanish-American War was precipitated, in part, by an explosion on board the USS Maine. Most likely the battleship blew up because of a faulty boiler, but its destruction was blamed on Spanish forces, leading bellicists to cry, "Remember the Maine, to Hell with Spain!"

3. **silentious (sigh-LENCH-us) (adj.):** Habitually taciturn. Harold Lloyd, now nearly forgotten, was once one of Hollywood's most famous silent comedians. Along with Charlie Chaplin and Buster Keaton, Lloyd ruled over Hollywood laughs during the silent era.

The fake word is:

torkmeat

Here are some additional terms/expressions from the Iraq War:

- Fallujah isn't just an Iraqi city; it's also slang for any place where everything is messed up and crawling with the enemy.
- FUBIJAR is a "sequel" to the World War II-era's FUBAR ("Fucked-Up Beyond All Recognition"). It means "Fucked-Up But I'm Just A Reservist."
- "Semper Fi," the Marines's motto, is short for the Latin expression "always faithful." "Semper Gumby," means "always flexible." Gumby is a flexible children's television character.

Safety Last!

Harold Clayton Lloyd Sr. (1893–1971) made almost two hundred movies during his career, which stretched from the silent and into the talkie era of Hollywood. He is best known for his silent film work, however.

One of his silent comedies, *Safety Last!* (a play on the expression "Safety first!"), is responsible for one of Hollywood's most enduring images. In the film, Lloyd climbs the "12-story Bolton Building" (really Los Angeles's ten-story International Savings & Exchange Bank Building). At one point, he winds up hanging from the hands of the building's clock, dangling over the street far below.

Lloyd performed most of the dangerous stunts in his movies, including this one, even though he had lost one of his thumbs due to a stunt mishap that occurred during the making of an earlier film.

---

fipple, argmonay, querela

1. **fipple (FIH-pull) (noun):** A grooved plug found at the end of an organ pipe, flute, or whistle. Another name for a whistle is an aerophone, an instrument that makes music via forced air.

2. **argmonay (ARG-muh-nay) (noun):** The name for the leftover wine not consumed during the Eucharist in Roman Catholic churches. Since Catholics believe this wine truly is the blood of Christ, priests consume the argmonay during Mass.

3. **querela (kwuh-REAL-uh) (noun):** An action in a court. A Virginia man sued himself in 1995 because he wished to be transferred from prison to a mental institution. Robert Lee Brock sued himself on grounds that he committed a crime while drunk, and drinking is against his religious beliefs. Therefore, he violated his own civil rights. A judge threw out this frivolous suit.

The fake word is:

argmonay

Most sacramental wine is produced at vineyards solely charged with making wine for religious purposes. Often, these wineries are run by priests or by members of religious orders.

America's oldest "sacramental vineyard" is O-Neh-Da Vineyard in New York's Finger Lakes region. Founded in 1872 by Bishop Bernard McQuaid, O-Neh-Da also makes table wine under the name Eagle Crest Vineyards. The "sinful wine" helps sustain operations of O-Neh-Da Vineyard.

Sue Me!

Frivolous lawsuits are one of the world's favorite pastimes!

- A Spanish businessman named Tomas Delgado hit and killed a seventeen-year-old boy who was riding his bicycle at night. He then sued the boy's family for damage their dead son did to his car!
- Vinicios Robacher, 15, of Connecticut sued his teacher for waking him up. The educator, irritated that Robacher was sleeping in class, slammed her hand down on his desk to wake him. The boy claimed the slam caused him permanent hearing damage.
- The mayor of Batman, a city in Turkey, sued *The Dark Knight* director for using his city's name without permission. And, yes, there really is a city named Batman in Turkey.
- Do you remember John Cage's "4'33"," a piece of "music" that consists of that amount of silence? Well, you may not think it's a legitimate "song," but the late Cage's publishers do. They sued musician Mike Batt for plagiarism, claiming his piece "A Minute's Silence" rips off Cage's four-plus minutes of silence.

kwinline, dwaible, hercogamous

1. **kwinline** (KWIHN-line) (noun): Synthetic fiber used in ladies' dresses since the 1960s. Kwinline is not shiny like some synthetic fabrics, but it rarely needs ironing and lasts longer than most clothing made from natural fibers.

2. **dwaible** (DWAY-bull) (adj.): Feeble, shaky, unstable on one's feet. If you've worked too hard for too long, then you're going to be a tad dwaible. The word also suggests the motion of the stereotypical zombie.

3. **hercogamous** (her-KAHG-uh-muss) (adj.): Incapable of self-fertilization. Most plants are "hermaphrodites" with both "male" parts (androecium) and "female" parts (gynoecium).

The fake word is:
kwinline

No one can brag about having a kwinline outfit because it doesn't exist, but no one would *want* to brag about having a polyester outfit either—and those do exist.

Polyethylene terephthalate (PET), known generically as polyester, is a polymer that can be composed of natural and/or human-made components. It's used to make "plastic" bottles, film, insulation, and to provide a high-gloss finish on wood products.

But for most people, polyester will always be associated with the height of 1970s decadence: leisure suits, disco dresses, etc. Perhaps due to this connection, the word "polyester" is practically a synonym for "bad taste."

They Won't Stay Dead!

Zombies "existed" prior to 1968. In Haiti, for example, the concept of someone who is undead (or, most likely, in a deep hypnotic state) due to a wizard's actions goes back centuries. Nonetheless, 1968 is the year that zombies became an indelible icon of popular culture because that's the year George A. Romero's *Night of the Living Dead* was first released.

The black and white film, made for a little more than $100,000, still has the power to shock audiences today, and has grossed around $20 million since its initial release. In the movie, radiation from a crashed space probe has turned the recently dead into the "living dead," dwaible corpses that feed on living human brains.

The film's success is due, in part, to its timeliness. It fed on fears of nuclear disasters (radioactive space probes), the government not being on the up-and-up (radioactive space probes), and mob mentality ('60s countercultural revolution).

---

koel, malch, connochaetes

1. **koel (CO-uhl) (noun):** A long-tailed cuckoo, native to India and Australia. Koels, like peacocks and peahens, are sexually dimorphic; that is, the males and females of the species look different. Not to be confused with Kohl's, a department store featuring cheap stuff for males and females of the human species.

2. **malch (MALTCH) (verb):** To prepare a field or course for game play. Groundskeepers for Major League Baseball can make $85,000 or more. Folks who take care of Little League fields, not so much.

3. **connochaetes (kahn-uh-KEED-eez) (noun):** The genus that comprises gnus. A gnu and a wildebeest are the same thing. Children may not like gnus because they kill Simba's father in Disney's *The Lion King*.

The fake word is:
malch

Biochemists were arguably more important than groundskeepers in 1966, a few years after major league baseball first moved to Texas.

The Astrodome, the first indoor, domed stadium in the major leagues, couldn't have "real" grass. The ballpark tried, but the glare from windows in the dome annoyed fans. After painting over some of the windows, the natural grass died. Fortunately, Donald Elbert, James Faria, and Robert Wright had invented Chemgrass in 1965. The synthetic green carpet-like "grass" sort of, kind of, resembled real grass. After it was put into the Astrodome in 1966, Chemgrass was renamed AstroTurf.

In 2000, the Astros moved outdoors to Enron Field, which became Minute Maid Park after the downfall of Enron. Humidity continues to be curbed during Astros games because the park's stadium has a retractable roof. And those Texas-sized mosquitoes? Maybe they got tired of being hit by line drives and buzzed off.

Kohl's, Not Koels

Now the nation's twenty-fourth largest retailer, Kohl's only become a national presence at the end of the last century. Max Kohl opened his first grocery store in 1946 in Wisconsin. He expanded his operation in 1962 to include an all-purpose department store in Brookfield, Wisconsin.

Ten years later, British American Tobacco bought a controlling interest in Kohl's. They eventually jettisoned the grocery stores to focus on department stores, which Max Kohl originally envisioned as being a cross between high-end and low-end retail. The company now has more than 1,000 stores across the United States.

dursheen, agelast, diglot

1. **dursheen (duhr-SHEEN) (noun):** A child left homeless by war or natural disaster. The number of orphans left by World War II is in dispute. Numbers range from one million to thirteen million.

2. **agelast (AJ-uh-last) (noun):** One who never laughs. A mirthless person. It's the opposite of an "abderian," or a person who laughs too much.

3. **diglot (DIG-laht) (noun):** Someone who can speak more than one language. It's related to the Greek *glottos*, meaning tongue.

The fake word is:
dursheen

Orphans—whether bereft of parents by war, disease, natural disaster, or poverty—often overcome their humble beginnings.

- Nelson Mandela was orphaned at age nine. He went on to win the Nobel Peace Prize, help to topple South Africa's racist apartheid system, and to become president of that country.
- Andrew Jackson went on to become a hero in the War of 1812 and the seventh president of the United States.
- Edgar Allan Poe's actor parents died when Poe was small, and he was raised by the Allan family. Poe had a fairly miserable life, it's true, but he has since his death come to be regarded as one of America's greatest and most innovative writers.
- Leo Tolstoy went on to become the author of two of the world's acknowledged literary masterpieces: *War and Peace* and *Anna Karenina*.

We Are Not Amused

Did Queen Victoria, monarch of Great Britain from 1837 until her death in 1901, ever actually say, "We are not amused"?

The statement is attributed to her by an early biographer, and is used as the quintessential example of the "royal we," or majestic plural. Nonetheless, no one is certain the queen ever actually said this or even if she meant "I" when she said "we." Perhaps, some have surmised, she was speaking for all the ladies in the room. Of course, one typically needs some sort of royal privilege to speak for everyone.

agonous, cultrivorous, mokey

1. **agonous** (AG-uh-nuss) (adj.): Having the characteristic of imposing pain on someone. There's a character in World of Warcraft called Agonous of the Undercity, which makes him a pretty agonous fighter.

2. **cultrivorous** (KUHL-tre-vor-us) (adj.): Characteristic of one swallowing knives. It can also mean "devouring" knives, but who wants to do that?

3. **mokey** (MOE-key) (adj.): Possessing an unusual gift, such as second sight. People display second sight in one of two ways. They either perceive visions of the future (precognition) or perceive events occurring at a distant location (remote viewing).

The fake word is:

mokey

We tend to associate clairvoyance with shady proprietors of home-based "fortune tellers," but one of America's most esteemed historical figures is believed (by some at least) to have been clairvoyant.

President Abraham Lincoln had a famous precognitive dream not long before his fatal appointment at Ford's Theater on April 14, 1865. The dream is written of in a memoir by Ward Hill Lamon, the president's bodyguard, who was not present with Lincoln at his assassination.

Lincoln told Lamon that, in his dream, he was walking through an eerily empty White House. In the distance, he could hear the sound of people weeping. When Lincoln got to the East Room, he saw a group of mourners surrounding a coffin on a raised platform. He could not determine the identity of the corpse. He asked the identity of the dead figure and was told that it was the president, who had been shot by an assassin.

"I slept no more that night," Lincoln told Lamon.

Mighty Tasty

Sword swallowers don't actually "swallow" swords, of course; they are basically just folks who are good at quelling their gag reflex.

Here's how it works. You put your head back, hyperextending your neck. Then, you have to learn to relax your upper esophageal sphincter (the thing that makes you gag). Next, move the lubricated sword (saliva is best) carefully past your pharynx. After that, it's easy—gravity will help the sword go down the flexible esophagus.

Do I really have to say that this is extremely dangerous—don't try it at home?

---

anglewitch, rintaster, bullimong

1. **anglewitch** **(ANG-el-WICH)** **(noun):** Bait, especially worms. It's also the name of a virtual-pet site on the Web, which is a really weird association.

2. **rintaster** **(RIHN-taste-uhr)** **(noun):** A cheese connoisseur. Rintasters have an expansive, specialized vocabulary to describe their affection for Brie.

3. **bullimong** **(BUL-e-mahng)** **(noun):** Cattle feed made from mixed-up grains. It comes from the Old English *gemong*, meaning a mixture of things.

The fake word is:

rintaster

There's no such thing as a rintaster, but an expansive, specialized vocabulary known only to the artisan cheese connoisseur does in face exist:

- affinage: The craft that involves aging and maturing cheese.
- cendre: Sprinkling cheese with dark vegetable ash.
- Penecillium candidum: A mold added to cheese to promote the growth of a bloomy, white rind.
- starter: Bacteria added to milk as the process of making cheese begins.
- toma: Semi-hard cow's milk cheese from Italy.

Now, That's Entertainment!

In Shakespeare's time, the theater was not a place for the hoity-toity. Prior to the curtain rising, spectators often enjoyed bear-baiting.

A bear was chained, by the leg or neck, to a stout post. Then, hunting dogs were released to fight the bear. If the bear wasn't chained, then there would be no contest. The "sport" continued until the bear died or the crowd ran out of dogs. Although this activity sounds horrifying to most of us today, bear-baiting was popular with the lowbrow and highbrow alike. King Henry VIII, he of the multitudinous wives, loved the sport and had a bear-baiting court put in at his palace. Even dour Queen Elizabeth I was a fan.

Bear-baiting still takes place in some countries, such as Pakistan. Local warlords organize the spectacles to test the mettle of their hunting dogs. Incidentally, the activity is outlawed in the Koran.

---

aucupate, xanterist, santir

1. **aucupate (AWK-you-pait) (verb):** From the Latin, to go birdwatching. It can also mean to lie in wait for, or to gain by craft.

2. **xanterist (ZAN-tuhr-ist) (noun):** A woman who dislikes other women. Named after Socrates's wife, Xanthippe.

3. **santir (san-TEE-uhr) (noun):** A Persian dulcimer played with curved sticks. Other stringed instruments used in Middle Eastern music include the qanoun, the oud, and the sitar.

The fake word is:

xanterist

Actually, Xanthippe (also written as Xantippe) *was* Socrates's wife, and her name is now used generically to describe a shrewish or "difficult" woman. Historians suggest that Xanthippe's reputation is unfounded. Certainly Plato, who wrote about his teacher Socrates, never cast aspersions on her character.

On the other hand, Xenophon, a contemporary of Socrates, puts negative words about Xanthippe into the mouth of her oldest son. Lamprocles complains of how harshly his mom treats him, but what kid *doesn't* complain about how "mean" his mother is?

Whether or not she was a bitch, her name has become synonymous with one ever since. In Shakespeare's *The Taming of the Shrew*, Petruchio compares Katherina (the shrew) to Xanthippe.

Rocking That Sitar

The one Middle Eastern instrument that rock fans may be familiar with is the sitar, thanks to the interest shown in it by George Harrison of The Beatles.

Harrison first experienced sitar music while on the set of *Help!*, the group's second film. He was inspired not only to learn to play the six-stringed, two-bridged instrument, but he also became interested in Eastern philosophy. Harrison took sitar lessons from Ravi Shankar, and the instrument first appeared in "Norwegian Wood (This Bird Has Flown)" on The Beatles album *Rubber Soul*.

After The Beatles used it, The Rolling Stones followed suit and put a sitar on "Paint It, Black." This opened the sitar floodgates. Other 1960s groups that used the sitar to add exotic sounds to their palettes include The Cyrkle, The Cowsills, and The Monkees.

wentus, palliasse, quarrion

1. **wentus (WHEN-tuss) (noun):** A needle-shaped ship, used by blockade runners during the American Civil War. The word is a corrupted form of the Latin "ventus," which means wind.

2. **palliasse (puh-LEE-as) (noun):** A pallet; also, a support for masonry work. Pallets, straw-filled mattresses on hard surfaces, were originally built for medieval servants.

3. **quarrion (kwah-REE-uhn) (noun):** A cockatiel. Yet another name for the quarrion/cockatiel is the weiro. Whatever you call it, this Australian bird is a popular pet.

The fake word is:

wentus

Blockade runners first emerged during the Peloponnesian War. They are associated today with piracy and drug trafficking, and they have been used in all modern wars. Nonetheless, for most fans of history "blockade runner" will always call to mind the Civil War.

From the war's outset, the Union understood that there were two keys to winning the Civil War: take control of the Mississippi River and keep Southern ports from getting overseas goods and weapons. The so-called Anaconda Plan was ultimately successful. The Union blockaded twelve major ports and patrolled more than 3,000 miles of coastland.

A blockade runner's job was to circumvent the patrolling Union ships and get much-needed supplies to the Confederacy. The task was dangerous, but it could also make good blockade runners wealthy due to kickbacks, overcharging, and other less-than-patriotic business methods. By the end of the Civil War, the Union captured or destroyed nearly 1,500 blockade vessels.

A Lot of Cockatiel Facts

First off, cockatiels are a type of parrot. They have common bills and feet, and can be taught to mimic human speech. Cockatiels are native to Australia, and they can live up to twenty-five years. Males are better parents. In the wild, female cockatiels sometimes fly off and abandon their young; males, by contrast, take care of their young and can be formidable enemies if their chicks are threatened. Cockatiels generally sell for anywhere from $40 to $140.

ryot, norn, squant

1. **ryot** (RIGH-uht) (noun): A peasant or tenant farmer in India. Yes, the word is pronounced the same as "riot." The mind boggles. If a bunch of ryots got together and protested something, it would be a ryot riot.

2. **norn** (NO-uhrn) (noun): A goddess ruling one's personal destiny. Norns are the Norse version of The Fates.

3. **squant** (SKWAHNT) (verb): To search; to do reconnaissance. The word is rarely used nowadays, but it was popular in the early days of American exploration. It is derived from Tisquantum, a Patuxet, better known to us as Squanto.

The fake word is:

squant

Tisquantum was captured by one of John Smith's lieutenants in 1614 and taken to England, where he was to be sold as a slave to the Spanish. Some Christian bigwigs halted this act, and Tisquantum was educated in Christian ways. Eventually, he was allowed to return home.

Tisquantum made it to Newfoundland, couldn't get passage to New England, went back to England, and finally made it back to present-day Massachusetts in 1619. He probably wished he hadn't bothered.

Tisquantum found that the Patuxets were practically extinct. Like many other tribes before them, the Patuxets were decimated by European diseases for which they had no natural immunity. Despite this, Tisquantum befriended the Europeans and helped them to survive New England's harsh winters.

Is It Fate?

The Moirae, better known as The Fates, are the Greek and Roman incarnations of destiny. They control the lives of every man, woman, and god. From various numbers, mythological history whittled them down to three.

- Clotho (Greek) or Nona (Roman) spins the thread of life.
- Lachesis (Greek) or Decima (Roman) measures the length of the thread of life for each person.
- Atropos (Greek) or Morta (Roman) is the cutter of the thread of life. She determines the method of each person's death.

shrum, booboisie, threap

1. **shrum (SHRUHM) (noun):** A loose tooth. "Baby teeth" are also known as deciduous or milk teeth.

2. **booboisie (boob-wahz-EE) (noun):** The class made up of those considered boobs, or fools. This neologism, comprised of the words "boob" and "bourgeoisie," was coined by journalist and critic H. L. Mencken.

3. **threap (THREEP) (verb):** To scold or chide; to contradict. The word comes from the Old English *threapian*, which means "to blame."

The fake word is:

shrum

In an eighteenth-century French fairy tale, a mouse turns into a fairy and hides under an evil king's pillow. In the middle of the night, the mouse knocks out the evil king's teeth. Thus, the "tooth fairy" was born.

The tooth fairy that we know today began to appear around the turn of the twentieth century. She takes baby teeth and replaces them with gifts, usually money. Since the 1980s, she has become a marketing phenomenon for whom special pillows, dolls, and piggy banks are designed.

The American Dental Association has determined that the average gift left by the tooth fairy is one dollar.

You (Oxy)Moron!

Contradictions sometimes hide larger truths. That seems to be the basis of the typical oxymoron anyway.

- **Living dead:** Zombies, vampires, and other "things" that imitate the living even though they're dead.
- **Virtual reality:** It looks so real, but it's fake! So, it's virtually reality.
- **Pianoforte:** Piano means soft. Forte means loud. Which one is it anyway?
- **Jumbo shrimp:** Well, we call these tasty little sea creatures shrimp. Sometimes, restaurants have really big ones, so you get the seemingly contradictory "jumbo shrimp."
- **Deafening silence:** Someone says something so ridiculous that it causes silence to flood the room. The silence is so oppressive that it is extremely noticeable.
- **Plastic glass:** We often call tumblers "glasses," and if they're made of plastic, then they're plastic glasses.

---

cockapert, gorn, churrasco

1. **cockapert (COCK-uh-puhrt) (adj.):** Impudent. Fans of *Little House on the Prairie* love to hate that cockapert vixen, "Naughty" Nellie Oleson.

2. **gorn (GORN) (noun):** A sudden glance. Flirtation often starts with gorns.

3. **churrasco (chew-RASS-koe) (noun):** Beef broiled on a spit over an open flame. When you think of the Wild West, you might think of cowboys around the fire, waiting to enjoy some churrasco. Or, if you're a fan of Mel Brooks's *Blazing Saddles*, you'll picture cowboys sitting around the fire polluting the wide open spaces with flatulence.

The fake word is:

gorn

Flirtation often starts with "gorns" . . . if you are in certain countries. In others, a flirtatious glance could mark you as a prostitute.

In the United States and in most European countries, glances between men and women are construed as harmless flirting. In most Muslim countries, however, men and women are not supposed to make prolonged eye contact because it is considered adulterous. If a Muslim man stares at a Western woman and she returns his glance, then he may consider her tacitly accepting a sexual offer.

Naughty Times Three

Alison Arngrim played Nellie Oleson for seven full seasons of the television version of Laura Ingalls Wilder's *Little House on the Prairie* series. But in Wilder's books, Nellie Oleson was based on three different people.

Nellie Owens was the basis for Nellie Oleson in *On the Banks of Plum Creek*. Owens's parents ran the local mercantile in Walnut Grove, just like Nellie Oleson's parents. Genevieve Masters was the real-life figure who had the most in common with Arngrim's character. She was, according to Wilder, spoiled, wore fine clothes, and had striking blonde hair. She was actually more unpleasant than television's Nellie Oleson, who loses some of her impudence as she matures. Masters is the model for the Nellie Oleson of *Little Town on the Prairie*.

Real-life Stella Gilbert was the model for the Nellie Oleson of *These Happy Golden Years*. She was Laura Ingalls's main rival for the affections of Almanzo Wilder.

---

dictature, kady, clampse

1. **dictature (dick-TAY-churr) (noun):** Office of a dictator or a body of dictators. So, if Stalin, Hitler, and Mussolini were hanging out at Starbucks, they wouldn't be a kaffeeklatsch, they'd be a dictature.

2. **kady (KAY-dee) (noun):** A man's hat, such as a straw hat or bowler. Before they became associated in the popular imagination with dark suits and sunglasses, FBI agents were known by their conspicuous straw hats.

3. **clampse (CLAMPSE) (verb):** To create a dystopian world, either in reality or in fiction. Literature is filled with those who clampse: George Orwell, Aldous Huxley, Philip Roth.

The fake word is:
clampse

In a dystopian novel, things have fallen apart badly, often because the government has become totalitarian. The best-known dystopian novel is George Orwell's *1984*, but it's hardly the only one. In fact, younger readers may only know "Big Brother" as the name of some reality show; they'll be more familiar with Lois Lowry's *The Giver*.

Winner of the 1994 Newbery Medal (the "Pulitzer" of young adult books), Lowry's book is about a society that believes it's utopian while, in fact, it's dystopian. *The Giver*'s world has eliminated pain and disharmony through "sameness."

Hoover's Dirt

J. Edgar Hoover was the first director of the Federal Bureau of Investigation and kept that position for nearly fifty years. One way he ensured a lengthy tenure was by keeping copious files on the salacious peccadillos of those who might fire him. Ironically, Hoover himself may have had much to hide.

Historians conjecture that Hoover may have been gay, something that would not have been deemed acceptable during most of the director's career. As far back as the 1940s, some believed that Hoover, who never married, was linked romantically with Clyde Tolson, the FBI's associate director. The two frequently vacationed together, and Tolson inherited Hoover's estate. In addition, some sources—possibly with axes to grind—reported that they attended homosexual parties at Hoover's home, during which Hoover dressed in women's clothes.

---

collieshangie, luctus, donsie

1. **collieshangie (KAHL-ee-shan-ee) (noun):** A squabble, brawl, or uproar. It's the Scottish equivalent to the Irish word "donnybrook."

2. **luctus (LUCK-tuss) (adj.):** Of or relating to the common or mundane. Fans of science fiction describe people who dislike sci-fi as luctus because non-fans are more interested in the mundane than in the possibilities of fantastic worlds.

3. **donsie (DAHN-see) (adj.):** Depending on the dialect, this word can mean unlucky, fastidious, quick-tempered, or sickly. Roderick Usher, of Edgar Allan Poe's "The Fall of the House of Usher" actually incorporates most of these various meanings. The protagonist is sickly and unlucky, fastidious, and quick-tempered—and he might also be guilty of an incestuous relationship with his sister.

The fake word is:

luctus

Mundane may be, well, mundane, but it's begun to get a lot of mileage—as a noun—from people who dabble in alternative realities. As noted, science fiction fans who really get into their realms of fantasy and space call people who eschew sci-fi "mundanes." Science fiction fans aren't alone, however. Re-enactors, those people who take history really seriously, call people who prefer getting their history from a textbook "mundanes."

That's Some Festival

The word "donnybrook" just sounds too nice to mean a knock-down, drag-out brawl. The word sounds like the fictional name some Svengali would give to a teen idol. The word is derived from a fair held for centuries in Dublin's Donnybrook district. In 1204, England's King John granted Dublin the right to hold an eight-day fair. Eventually, the fair's length was extended to fifteen days.

Now, when you think of "fair" you might think of midway games and thrill rides designed to make children throw up. Well, the Donnybrook Fair had plenty of throwing up, but that's because its main purpose was drinking copious amount of alcohol and getting into brutal fights. Public outcry eventually forced the city of Dublin to buy the fair's license in order to end the Donnybrook once and for all in 1855.

---

spruiker, blimsie, towmond

1. **spruiker (SPROOK-uhr) (noun):** A barker, as at a carnival. Elvis Presley's manager, "Colonel" Tom Parker (the title was an honorary one), served as a carnival barker prior to his involvement with talent management. Parker also—rumor has it—painted common birds yellow and sold them to suckers as canaries in order to make money.

2. **blimsie (BLIHM-zee) (adj.):** Of or related to unpredictable behavior, especially when such behavior is related to drunkenness. Beat Generation author Jack Kerouac's 1968 appearance on William F. Buckley's *Firing Line* was a bit blimsie.

3. **towmond (TOE-muhnd) (noun):** Twelve months; a year. From the Middle English "towlmonyth."

The fake word is:
blimsie

Conservative icon William F. Buckley was a friend of counterculture pioneer Jack Kerouac who, ironically, was never comfortable being considered counterculture. Most people didn't realize that the freewheeling Dean Moriarty, in Kerouac's immortal *On the Road*, was based on Neal Cassady and not on the relatively staid, conservative Kerouac.

In 1968, a seemingly drunk and older-than-his-years Kerouac appeared on Buckley's show. The subject? Hippies. Kerouac didn't like 'em. He didn't even like his old friend, Allen Ginsberg, who had been "adopted" by the hippies. At one point on the show, the incredibly fidgety Kerouac gave a "thumbs down" to Ginsberg, who was in the audience. "He's a nice fella," Kerouac said. "Yeah, we'll feed him to the lions."

Colonel Tom . . . van Kuijk?

Colonel Tom Parker probably didn't have much trouble lying to passersby during his days as a carnival barker. After all, his entire identity was a lie.

"Tom Parker" was born Andreas Cornelis van Kuijk in the Netherlands, and he entered the United States illegally. He joined the peacetime army—which must not have been too big on screening recruits in those days—and took the name Tom Parker from an officer who recruited him.

lomonthe, pliskie, joukery

1. **lomonthe (low-MAHNTH-uh) (noun):** A spirit guide or one's spiritual alter ego. Long before folks like James Van Praagh and John Edwards (the "medium," not the adulterous politician), a Nobel Prize-winning poet had his own spirit guide who served as an invisible best friend.

2. **pliskie (PLIH-ski) (noun):** A practical joke. Shows featuring jokes played on celebrities have long been popular: *Candid Camera*, *Punk'd*, etc. Iraqi television took the concept to a whole new level in 2010 with a show in which fake bombs are planted in the cars of Iraqi celebrities. The cars are stopped at checkpoints, the "bombs" found, and soldiers threaten to send the hapless celebrity to prison or execution.

3. **joukery (JOOK-uh-ree) (noun):** Swindling or trickery. A joukery in chess is a trick played on a stronger opponent that causes the "tricker" to win or draw instead of facing a certain loss.

The fake word is:
lomonthe

William Butler Yeats, who won the Nobel Prize for literature in 1923, was an avid spiritualist who made a good "friend" at a séance in 1914. When Yeats "met" Leo Africanus, who shuffled off this mortal coil in the sixteenth century, it didn't start off well. Africanus was a Moor who wrote a book about the geography of North Africa. He claimed to be incensed that Yeats hadn't heard of him. The two got to know each other, and Africanus even "helped" Yeats by working through him during automatic writing sessions. "Automatic writing" involves someone supposedly writing without conscious thought, while being led by a spirit guide.

Swindle King

The king of chess swindlers was Frank Marshall. He was one of the early twentieth century's strongest players, but this didn't stop him from attempts to pull the rug out from under his opponents.

A chess swindle typically involves a player making an unexpected and contrary move. The result is to confuse an opponent. In a sense, it's like bluffing during poker. Marshall became such a consummate swindler that, to this day, tricky chess players are accused of "Marshall swindles."

mirligoes, primatist, sleechy

1. **mirligoes (MUHR-lee-goes) (noun):** Vertigo or dizziness. Many consider Alfred Hitchcock's *Vertigo* (1958) not only the master director's best film but also one of the best films ever made. Ironically, *Vertigo* received mixed reviews and lackluster box office when first released. With the exception of two nominations in technical categories, "Oscar" snubbed the film as well.

2. **primatist (PRIME-uh-tist) (noun):** One who keeps a monkey as a pet. The practice had been considered "cute" until Travis, a chimpanzee who appeared in commercials and on television shows, seriously injured a friend of his owner.

3. **sleechy (SLEE-chee) (adj.):** Oozy or slimy. The sleechy used car salesman is just a modern variation on the fairy and folk tale tradition of characterizing peddlers as "bad guys" out to corrupt good people. Think, for example, of the man who trades "Jack" some "magic beans" for the family's cow.

The fake word is:
primatist

The only pet monkey we know won't seriously injure someone is Curious George.

The inquisitive monkey who often gets into trouble before making things right was "born" in 1941. His "parents" were Hans Augusto (a.k.a. "H. A.") Rey and his wife, Margret Rey. In *Curious George*, the monkey's curiosity gets him caught by the never-named Man with the Yellow Hat, who takes him back home to "the big city." Six more adventures by the original husband and wife team followed.

Acrophobia Just Doesn't Sound As Good

In Hitchcock's *Vertigo*, Jimmy Stewart's character actually suffers from acrophobia, or fear of heights. Vertigo and acrophobia often are confused. Vertigo is the sensation of spinning or whirling when one is stationary. It can be caused by "dizzying" heights, but it also—and more often—is caused by drinking too much.

---

dolioform, hunth, remite

1. **dolioform (DOE-lee-uh-form) (adj.):** Shaped like a barrel. In the United States, all whiskey—with the exception of corn whiskey—must be aged at least two years in oak barrels.

2. **hunth (HUNTH) (abbreviation):** An abbreviation for hundred thousand. The next time you're in Ireland, give others a cheery "Cead Mile Failte," which is Gaelic for "A Hundred Thousand Welcomes."

3. **remite (REE-mite) (verb):** To temporarily blind an animal while hunting it. Deer, for example, have a tendency to, well, act like a "deer in the headlights" and freeze when a sudden light is shined into their eyes. Unscrupulous hunters sometimes take advantage of this fact and remite their quarry.

The fake word is:

remite

In modern times, few have so mastered the art of appearing like a deer in the headlights quite like Dan Quayle. If you've forgotten him, that's okay—he was the eminently forgettable vice president to the first President Bush. When he wasn't castigating fictional characters for choosing to have a child out of wedlock (the character was Murphy Brown from the show of the same name), Quayle was busy looking and acting clueless. Here are just a few highlights:

- "I have made good judgments in the past. I have made good judgments in the future."
- "Republicans understand the importance of bondage between a mother and child."
- "What a waste it is to lose one's mind. Or not to have a mind is being very wasteful. How true that is."
- "The Holocaust was an obscene period in our nation's history. I mean in this century's history. But we all lived in this century. I didn't live in this century."

Show Me the Way to the Next Whiskey Barrel

Whiskey is aged in oak barrels for three reasons. First off, oak has natural properties that add to a whiskey's taste and aroma. Secondly, oak helps remove some of the unwanted elements, such as sulfur, in the spirit. Finally, it helps to change some of the chemical compounds in the spirit, making it tastier for human consumption.

murgeon, vankler, iceblink

1. **murgeon (MUHR-juhn) (noun):** A grimace; or, complaints. Ronald McDonald, now apparently the sole occupant of McDonaldland, once had a bunch of buddies. One of them was named Grimace, an amorphous-shaped purple monster who began life as a shake-stealing villain before being transformed into a good guy.

2. **vankler (VANK-luhr) (noun):** A busybody. You know the type, and you go running when you see one.

3. **iceblink (ICE-BLINK) (noun):** Sometimes written as two words, an iceblink is a white light on the underside of clouds caused by reflections off of a field of ice. The Inuit (a.k.a. Eskimo) and European explorers used iceblinks to help navigate the Northwest Passage, a sea route through the Arctic Ocean.

The fake word is:
vankler

Gladys Kravitz has a special place in the pantheon of busybody neighbors. She has been featured in an episode of *Family Guy* and *The Simpsons*, and Indie band The Tories featured her in one of their songs. She has come to be a synonym for "nosy person."

Prior to her place in pop culture history, she was a thorn in the side of Samantha and Darrin Stephens. Gladys always seemed to catch Samantha, the comely witch and featured character in *Bewitched*, performing feats of magic. "Abner!" Gladys would scream to her husband. He would just ignore her.

Farewell, McDonaldland

From the early 1970s until the dawn of the twenty-first century, McDonald's featured McDonaldland and its wacky characters in its advertising campaigns. Children today may be somewhat familiar with the characters because they're still painted on the walls of some McDonald's PlayPlaces, but alas, the characters have been phased out . . . with the exception of spokesclown Ronald McDonald.

In addition to Grimace, similar in demeanor and intelligence to SpongeBob's buddy Patrick Starfish, McDonaldland was led by genial Mayor McCheese (a well-dressed individual with a cheeseburger for a head), protected by Officer Big Mac (sporting a spiffy constable's uniform and a bobby's hat atop his Big Mac head), and sometimes imperiled by the Hamburglar (dressed in black-and-white stripes, a red cape, and a mask).

---

blowth, staggie, wuntle

1. **blowth (BLOWTH) (noun):** In the blooming stage. The word is pretty obscure, but Sir Walter Raleigh liked to use it. He would write of flora being "in the blowth and bud."

2. **staggie (STAG-ee) (noun):** A colt. The Scots call them this, most likely, because colts have a tendency to stagger a bit when first born.

3. **wuntle (ONE-tull) (verb):** To waddle like a duck. The word was created by Edward Lear, the second-best writer of nonsense verse who ever lived. (Lewis Carroll is first.)

The fake word is:
wuntle

Lear may not have made up wuntle, but he was a fount of neologisms. One of his favorites is "runcible," which most famously appears in his most famous poem, "The Owl and the Pussycat": "They dined on mince, and slices of quince / Which they ate with a runcible spoon."

Lear never actually tells us what a "runcible spoon" is, but many have come to the conclusion that it's akin to a spork, that super awesome spoon-fork hybrid thingy you'll find at KFC. However, this assumption may be incorrect. Lear, who was also an artist, once drew a picture of the dolomphious (another neologism) duck using a runcible spoon, and the object looks just like a ladle.

The Lost Colony

When he wasn't busy writing of "blowths and buds," Sir Walter Raleigh tried to settle the Colony and Dominion of Virginia, which includes present-day Virginia and North Carolina. Most famously, he attempted to establish a settlement on North Carolina's Roanoke Island.

The settlers mysteriously disappeared, leaving only the word "CROATOAN" as a clue. The name of a local tribe misspelled, "CROATOAN" might have meant the settlers were slaughtered by the Croatan, removed by the Croatan, or simply assimilated into the tribe. The hapless settlers' and Raleigh's effort to gain a toehold in the New World have come to be called "The Lost Colony of Roanoke Island."

---

blastage, oneirocritic, kellion

1. **blastage (BLAST-uhj) (noun):** A tunnel created by blasting with an explosive. Often, caves marketed as tourist attractions require the creation of some blastages in order to create enough head room for the general public.

2. **oneirocritic (oh-NEE-row-criht-ihc) (noun):** One who interprets dreams. Dream interpretation has probably existed since people have existed, but one of the earliest literary examples of dream interpretation takes place in the Epic of Gilgamesh. Gilgamesh dreams of an axe falling from the sky, and his mother becomes Gilgamesh's oneirocritic. Her interpretation? The axe suggests someone will come into Gilgamesh's life. The two will fight, ultimately become friends, and accomplish great things.

3. **kellion (kih-LEE-uhn) (noun):** A small house used by members of the Eastern Church. So-called Eastern Christianity begins with the division between the Western and Eastern Roman Empire.

The fake word is:

blastage

"Show" caves, those open to the public, really do sometimes have to resort to blasting passages in order to make their caverns accessible to the general public.

History doesn't record whether or not the first show cave used explosives. A written record from 1213 B.C. discusses a tour of Postojna Cave in Slovenia. The Chinese created the first explosives in the tenth century.

Postojna Cave is still open to tourists today.

Modern-Day Dream Interpretation

You don't need an oneirocritic to interpret dreams. You just need Google:

- Losing your teeth in a dream can foretell a financial windfall, or it can suggest that you are facing something you fear will be humiliating and/or embarrassing.
- Snake dreams suggest you are being hounded by hidden, recurring fears.
- Dreams about death, while terrifying, usually just mean that you are facing a huge life change. For example, you might have a dream about death just before you get married or take on your first "real" job.
- Dreams of pregnancy, if you are not pregnant, usually symbolize some part of your life that is growing or developing: a new romance, a new career move, etc.
- Water dreams are particularly telling. If the water in your dream is clear, then you're feeling in tune with your spiritual self. If your water is dirty, then you are totally hung up, dude.

ramular, transile, uranian

1. **ramular (RAM-yuh-luhr) (adj.):** Of or relating to a branch. A tree branch, to a botanist, is a ramus. Large branches are called boughs, while small branches are known as twigs. Babies should not be rocked in treetops because boughs have a tendency to break.

2. **transile (TRAN-sile) (adj.):** Of or related to animals with prehensile lips. Orangutans, horses, rhinos, and lake sturgeons are transile.

3. **uranian (you-RAIN-ee-uhn) (noun):** A common term, used in the nineteenth century, for a homosexual. Initially, it referred to the so-called third sex, defined as a female psyche in a male body. Oscar Wilde proudly accepted his role as a uranian: "To have altered my life would have been to have admitted that Uranian love is ignoble. I hold it to be noble."

The fake word is:

transile

In case you're not familiar with the term, "prehensile" refers to appendages on animals that have adapted for grasping and holding. You might, for instance, have heard of a "prehensile tail." Monkeys have these; they allow them to hang from trees.

In addition to tails, lips really can be prehensile, even though there's no such word as transile. So can noses: elephants, tapirs. Giraffes have prehensile tongues, which help them grab leafy dinners off trees. Finally, an octopus's arms are prehensile.

What Kind of Parent ARE You?

The familiar nursery rhyme "Rock-a-Bye Baby" first appeared in *Mother Goose's Melody* (1765), though it's probably much older. If you think about it, the song is pretty freaking creepy. Who would rock a baby in a treetop? Well, there are various theories to answer that question.

Perhaps the rhyme was written by an English immigrant to the American colonies, who witnessed a Native American woman actually rocking her baby in a treetop.

Local legend in Derbyshire, England, states that the "rocker" is Betty Kenny, an eccentric local woman who rocked her babies in the hollowed-out bough of a tree.

Or, perhaps the rhyme is an allegory for events surrounding the Revolution of 1688, also known as the Glorious Revolution, which led to the overthrow of King James II of England. The wind blowing is the wind of revolutionary change . . . or something like that.

janeite, agrostology, grestine

1. **janeite (JAYN-ite) (noun):** A Jane Austen fanatic. Austen may only have published four novels in her lifetime—and anonymously at that—but she has become one of the contemporary world's most popular purveyors of "classic literature."

2. **agrostology (ag-ruh-STALL-uh-jee) (noun):** Botanic branch dealing with grasses. Grass belongs to the Poaceae family. There are 10,000 or more distinctive species of grass. Put that in your pipe and smoke it.

3. **grestine (GREH-steen) (noun):** The formal name for a ten-gallon hat. While it's true that the Stetson hat company once boasted that the tight weave of its hats allowed them to hold water, the company also admits that a "ten-gallon hat" can only hold three gallons.

The fake word is:
grestine

If it doesn't actually hold ten gallons, then how did this classic cowboy hat get its name?

The prevailing theory is that the word "gallon" is a corruption of the Spanish "galon" or "galloon," which describes the braided trimming that goes around the base of the hat. When Spanish-speaking cowboys talked about their, uh, "*dix galon*" hats, they were referring to the proportion of the ribbons around their headgear. English-speaking cowboys "translated" the term into "ten-gallon" hat.

Not So Plain Jane

If we encounter something bizarre, we might tell friends the moment was "Felliniesque," after the surrealist filmmaker Federico Fellini. If we witness something dark or scary and bizarre, then we might call the experience "Kafkaesque," after the author Franz Kafka. But those who refer to Jane Austen typically refer to her on a first-name basis: janeite (or Janeite).

If sharp-eyed janeites noticed that I left off two of the author's six books, they're right. *Northanger Abbey* and *Persuasion* were not published until after Austen's death—possibly from Addison's disease, possibly from Hodgkin's lymphoma—in 1817. Ironically, *Northanger Abbey*, a parody of gothic fiction, was Austen's first completed novel.

---

indige, dobla, spannerman

1. **indige (in-DIJE) (verb):** To eat or drink to excess on a routine basis. Apparently, the word is a mix of "indulge" and "imbibe." With some thirty-two percent of American adults obese, the United States has one of the highest obesity rates in the world.

2. **dobla (DOE-bluh) (noun):** A gold coin once used by the Spanish. In 1985, modern-day treasure hunter Mel Fisher found the wreck of the *Nuestra Senora de Atocha* ("Our Lady of Atocha"), which had been lost with other ships in its fleet in 1622 near the Florida Keys. The Atocha offered a motherlode of jewelry, gold, and silver, estimated at somewhere north of half a billion dollars. Fisher fought Florida and the federal government for eight years before the Supreme Court ruled the treasure was his.

3. **spannerman (SPAN-uhr-man) (noun):** A (typically) blue-collar workman who uses a spanner. Americans call a spanner a wrench.

The fake word is:

indige

- The term "junk food" was coined in 1972 by Michael Jacobson, director of the Center for Science in the Public Interest. Junk food contains "empty calories" because the calories don't team up with any nutritional value.
- The opposite of junk food is whole foods. Whole foods are largely unprocessed and unrefined and contain few added ingredients.
- Comfort food is consumed to improve one's emotional status, but it probably won't work ultimately. If you consume a gallon of ice cream to cheer yourself up, you'll feel crappy later when you step onto the scale.

Am I Blue?

Manual laborers often get their clothes dirty at work, so blue has long been a favored color for work shirts. Blue, unlike white, hides some of the grime. In addition, many laborers wear blue coveralls containing the name of their company as well as their own name. All of this blue led to the term "blue-collar worker."

---

canikan, enginous, raffline

1. **canikan (CAN-ih-kan) (noun):** A small drinking vessel or can; in New England, it's a bucket, the sort you might find hanging over a wishing well.

2. **enginous (EN-juh-nuss) (adj.):** Put together with care; or, pertaining to an engine. The first self-propelled on-land vehicle was created in 1769 by France's Nicolas Joseph Cugnot. His steam-powered tractor could go a zephyr-like 2.5 miles per hour, and it had to stop every ten or fifteen minutes to build up steam power.

3. **raffline (RAFF-line) (noun):** Chiefly Canadian, it's a single word for "pick-up line."

The fake word is:
raffline

Unfortunately, cheesy pick-up lines are not. Well, they sort of are fake, in a way, but . . . whatever. Here are some egregious ones.

- Was that an earthquake, or did you just rock my world?
- I'm not a genie, but I can make your wishes come true.
- Baby, your body is a wonderland, and I want to be Alice.
- Be unique. Just say yes.
- I've just moved you to the top of my "to do" list.
- You must be tired from running through my dreams all night.
- Are you from Nashville? Because you're the only ten I see (Tennessee, get it?).

Who?!?

The first automobile powered by an internal combustion engine was invented by Francois Isaac de Rivaz.

After retiring from a life spent mostly in the French parliament, de Rivaz turned tinkerer. In 1807, he invented an internal combustion engine powered by hydrogen and oxygen. The next year, he devised a vehicle in which to place his engine. Unfortunately for de Rivaz's posterity, the engine didn't work all that well, and the "car" wasn't designed very well, so his invention was relegated to a footnote. Still, he paved the road for other, more successful, tinkerers.

gyascutus, duss, rakshasa

1. **gyascutus** (guy-us-KYOO-duss) (noun): An imaginary creature with two legs shorter than the others, making it walk along hillsides with ease. This critter is known by many other names as well: sidehill gouger, wowser, guadaphro, hunkus, gwinter, and cutter cuss.

2. **duss** (DUSS) (verb): To dance when one clearly does not know how to do so. A British team of researchers, focusing on men, figured out the great mystery of what makes bad dancing bad. It's all in the arms and legs. Literally. Bad dancers basically only move their arms and legs repetitively.

3. **rakshasa** (ROCK-shuh-suh) (noun): In Hindu mythology, an evil spirit or demon. Rakshasas also appear in the role-playing game Dungeons & Dragons as powerful sorcerers native to the Material Plane.

The fake word is:
duss

The good news for bad dancers is that the British researchers also determined what makes good dancing good. So, guys, if you want to impress the lay-tees, then pay attention.

The researchers filmed nineteen male volunteers offering their best moves, transformed the dancers into avatars, and had a team of thirty-seven women judge the results. Those deemed good dancers invariably put their torsos and necks into the dancing process.

Mmm, Haggis!

The gyascutus has a Scottish cousin called the wild haggis. This fictional creature also has one set of legs longer than the other. Those with longer left legs can run quickly around a mountain clockwise, while those with longer right legs are better at running counterclockwise.

Jokesters will claim the wild haggis is the central ingredient in haggis, Scotland's national dish. In fact, haggis is made up of a normally legged sheep's heart, liver and lungs, mixed with oatmeal and spices, and simmered in the animal's stomach for at least three hours. An acquired taste, indeed.

---

popskull, louster, krampt

1. **popskull (PAHP-SKULL) (noun):** Inferior, cheap whiskey. Cheap brands that people swear still taste good include Old Crow and Rebel Yell.

2. **louster (LOW [as in "now"]-stuhr) (verb):** To work actively; to bustle or scurry about. Since 1990, people have avoided loustering by playing solitaire. (That's the first year the game came standard with Microsoft Windows.)

3. **krampt (KRAMPT) (adj.):** Completely worn out, as by hard work. Who says you can't become krampt by playing several hands of solitaire online? Think of the stress you endure each time you think you're going to win—only to find that the computer has bested you again. Consider the joy of watching the cards bounce joyfully when you do win. Exhausting!

The fake word is:

krampt

The workweek, according to most people, sucks. Sure, we're all glad we have jobs, but do they have to be so taxing? The "average" workweek in the United States is Monday through Friday and lasts forty hours. In other countries, there are some variations.

- Bahrain's office workweek begins on Sunday and ends on Thursday. Weekends are Fridays, which are prayer days, and Saturdays. Other predominantly Muslim countries also have Friday-Saturday weekends.
- Indian workweeks add an extra half-day. Employees are on the clock from Monday through half of Saturday, so they put in an average of fifty hours per week.
- China, which Westerners may think of as keeping their workers on the floor 24/7, actually adopted the forty-hour workweek in 1995. Of course, that's just the *official* working hours.

Solitary Information

- The game most people think of as "solitaire" actually is called Klondike.
- The odds of winning aren't too bad. If you play correctly, the number of solvable games is between 82% and 91.5%.
- Microsoft's "Solitaire" first came standard with Windows 3.0, and it was developed by an intern named Wes Cherry. No, Cherry does not receive royalties for his invention.
- Avoid playing in New York. In 2006, New York City Mayor Michael Bloomberg fired a city employee who was caught playing Windows Solitaire during working hours.

---

nunter, fomorian, knodel

1. **nunter (NUN-tuhr) (verb):** To hide or to conceal evidence. Some cover-ups are legitimate: Watergate, the Iran-Contra Affair, the Dreyfus Affair. Some are the work of overactive imaginations: John F. Kennedy's assassination, the New World Order, UFO sightings.

2. **fomorian (FOE-more-ee-uhn) (noun):** A race of sea robbers in Celtic legends. Typically, these demi-gods are pictured as having the bodies of men and the heads of goats.

3. **knodel (kuh-NO-duhll) (noun):** A dumpling. Dumplings, whether made from potatoes, flour, bread, or matzoh, are a staple of world cuisine.

The fake word is:
nunter

For Woodrow Wilson or Sir Winston Churchill, "new world order" referred to an idealistic, post-war world of peace and understanding. For crackpots, the New World Order is something else entirely.

Theories differ but have certain commonalities. In general, the New World Order suggests that there is a group of global elites—polticians, billionaires, religious leaders—secretly plotting to replace all of the world's sovereign states with one authoritarian government.

If this reminds you of, say, *1984*, then you're right. The New World Order is fiction.

The Stuff of Nightmares

Some people actually believe in the New World Order, but nobody believes in formorians any longer. Nonetheless, linguistic researchers have figured out why these goat-headed creatures of Celtic legend are associated with the sea. It's all a big misunderstanding.

For many years, people believed the creatures' name derived from "muire," meaning "sea." Others suggested that one should look at the entire word. "Fo" means "under," and "muire" means "sea," so the fomorians are creatures who lived under the sea. Still others suggest the creature's name actually derives from an Old English word meaning "mare" and thus a fomorian is something you'd see in nightmares.

lithochromy, stookie, astrewn

1. **lithochromy (LITH-uh-krow-me) (noun):** The art of painting on stone. The earliest known examples are European cave paintings dating back 32,000 years.

2. **stookie (STOO-kee) (noun):** A fool. Picture Jerry Lewis, the American filmmaker Americans hate and the French love.

3. **astrewn (uh-STROON) (adj.):** Placed in a haphazard manner. Picture the average teenager's bedroom. Just don't ask too many questions.

The fake word is:

astrewn

If you're disorganized, there's hope! Here are several things you can start doing today that will help you become the most organized person you know.

- Do it now. Whatever it is. Don't procrastinate. You won't feel any more like doing the task later.
- Develop routines like cleaning the floor every time anything begins to accumulate on it.
- Have a place for everything, and put everything in its place.
- Pick up after yourself.
- Buy a personal organizer and actually use it.

Is He Better than Flatulence?

Jerry Lewis, as many know, is lionized by French critics as a genius. Americans scratch their collective heads. Perhaps you'll understand French esteem when you consider the country's love of low comedy, best exemplified by *le petomane* (the fart).

Joseph Pujol was a flatulist, or professional farter, who lived from 1857 to 1945. He was known as the Fartiste. Pujol had the ability to fart at will. He could mimic thunderstorms and cannon fire. He also had the ability to "play" such songs as "O Sole Mio" and the French national anthem, "La Marsellaise" on an instrument whose "playing end" was jammed into his anus. Now, *that's* genius.

tarre, bwert, wetfastness

1. **tarre** (TAR) (verb): To urge into action; incite. In 1968, the Youth International Party did its best to disrupt the 1968 Democratic National Convention. Democrats and Republicans alike would have been happy to "tarre" and feather Abbie Hoffman, Jerry Rubin, and the rest of their so-called "Groucho Marxists."

2. **bwert** (BWUHRT) (noun): The name for those lines comics artists draw that indicate something is moving at a high rate of speed. Mort Walker, creator of *Beetle Bailey*, invented an entire language for cartoonists, called Symbolia.

3. **wetfastness** (WET-fast-nuhss) (noun): Resistance to change when wet, as cloth or dye. One of the most popular waterproof fabrics used in coats is Gore-Tex. Its popularity is due to the fact that it's also breathable.

The fake word is:

bwert

Symbolia does, however, exist.

- A briffit is a little puff of dust in the spot recently occupied by a character that took off fast.
- If something is supposed to appear hot or smelly, cartoonists create wavy, rising lines called waftaroms.
- Agitrons are the wiggly lines that make a character look like it's shaking in fear.
- Plewds, which look like flying droplets of sweat, make a character look nervous.
- And those lines that make something look like it's moving quickly do have a name—two, in fact: blurgits and swallops.

── Goodbye, Mr. Hoffman ──

Abbie Hoffman was the crown prince of the Youth International Party (the Yippies), and he is one of the seminal figures of the 1960s. Unfortunately, he never seemed to continue on with his life once protesting stopped being *de rigueur*.

While other Yippies went on to become greedy, money-hungry yuppies, Hoffman continued his life of protest. His last book, *Steal This Urine Test*, was an amusing condemnation of the federal government's anti-drug policy, for example. Diagnosed with bipolar disorder, Hoffman died on April 12, 1989, after swallowing 150 Phenobarbital pills. He was only fifty-two.

telg, graith, dereem

1. **telg (TELG) (abbreviation):** An abbreviation for telegram. Western Union, once synonymous with telegrams, now focuses on financial services like money orders.

2. **graith (GRAYTH) (verb):** To prepare something for use; to put in order. One of the biggest lies in existence is "easy to assemble," sometimes printed on the boxes of children's prospective Christmas gifts.

3. **dereem (duh-REEM) (verb):** To make significant changes to a manuscript. Maxwell Perkins, considered the greatest editor in modern history, indeed made many significant changes to the work of novelist Thomas Wolfe.

The fake word is:

dereem

While at publisher Charles Scribner's Sons, Maxwell Perkins became the editor of F. Scott Fitzgerald, Ernest Hemingway, and Thomas Wolfe. But it was with Wolfe that Perkins is most associated.

Wolfe was famous for writing 10,000 words at a sitting, but he was not very self-disciplined when it came to self-editing. Perkins wound up cutting 90,000 words from Wolfe's first novel, *Look Homeward, Angel*. It became a huge bestseller. Wolfe's follow-up, *Of Time and River*, was even longer and required even more cutting.

So many people criticized Wolfe, suggesting the real genius behind his work was Perkins, that Wolfe "left" Perkins and Scribner's for another publisher. Wolfe died soon after. Wolfe's two posthumous novels, not usually considered to have the quality of his first two, were not worked on by Perkins.

Calling Western Union

For much of the twentieth century, Western Union was the favorite way for Americans to send messages fast. As such, it filtered its way into popular culture:

- When asked about the "message" of one of his films, producer Samuel Goldwyn replied, "Pictures are for entertainment, messages should be delivered by Western Union."
- The horrible leg lamp Ralphie's dad loves so much in *A Christmas Story* comes into the old man's possession thanks to a Western Union contest.
- The Five Americans recorded the song "Western Union" in 1967, and it reached number five on the charts.
- The 1941 film *Western Union* is a fictionalized account of the effort to build the transcontinental telegraph line.

Finster, regalo, bonspiel

1. **Finster (FIN-stuhr) (verb, usually capitalized):** To paint in a primitive style. The word is derived from Howard Finster, a "primitive artist" from Georgia who attained national popularity in the 1980s and 1990s.

2. **regalo (ruh-GAY-low) (noun):** A gift; a bonus; a treat. Even before the national economy began to tank, the majority of American companies stopped giving the traditional holiday bonus. According to a poll in 2005, 60 percent of America's companies didn't plan to offer holiday bonuses.

3. **bonspiel (BAHN-speel) (noun):** A curling match. Curling first became an Olympic sport in 1998.

The fake word is:
finster

Howard Finster (1916–2001) was a folk artist whose works tended to have a religious element since he had been "born again" as a teenager.

Finster worked in relative obscurity for most of his life, but then he was "discovered" by R.E.M., a band formed in Athens, Georgia. Finster and his home's sculpture garden were featured in the group's video for its first single, "Radio Free Europe."

Later, Finster drew the cover for R.E.M.'s second album, *Reckoning* (1984). In 1985, Finster drew the cover for Talking Heads's *Little Creatures* album.

Help! I Need Some Curling

Curling and the Olympics. Check! Curling and Canadians. Check! Curling and The Beatles. Screech. Huh? Yes, it's true.

The Fab Four's second film, *Help!*, was filmed in color and in multiple locations. One of them was the Austrian Alps. For one scene, you can see The Beatles curling the old-fashioned way, with stones and brooms.

A villain tries to kill the group by handing George Harrison a stone with a bomb hidden in it. Noticing the smoke, The Beatles run away. A hole is blown into the ice, and a swimmer pops up out of it, asking for directions to the White Cliffs of Dover.

curn, flintitious, scarrow

1. **curn (KERN) (noun):** A few; a small number. According to Harry Nilsson and Three Dog Night, one is the loneliest number that you'll ever do.

2. **flintitious (flin-TISH-us) (adj.):** Prone to being miserly. Ebenezer Scrooge is literature's most famously flintitious individual.

3. **scarrow (SKAH-row) (noun):** Faint or shadowy light. New York's Tin Pan Alley, once the nexus of music publishing, produced countless songs extolling scarrow, as produced by the moon.

The fake word is:

flintitious

Ebenezer Scrooge has lent his name to those who don't get into the Christmas spirit, but he's not the only fictional character to do so. The other is the Grinch.

Dr. Seuss unleashed the Grinch on the holiday public with 1957's *How the Grinch Stole Christmas*. In 1966, the Grinch became the star of a perennial Christmas television event. Voiced by horror film actor Boris Karloff, the Grinch discovers the true meaning of Christmas only after he has attempted to destroy the holiday for a bunch of unsuspecting little people called Whos.

Notice that both the Grinch and Scrooge are "rehabilitated" by the end of their stories, but the allusions to them refer to their lives prior to embracing the holiday spirit.

What Rhymes with Silver?

Tin Pan Alley's best-known "moon-June-balloon" song is 1909's "By the Light of the Silvery Moon," written by Gus Edwards and Edward Madden. In addition to "balloon" and "June," the song also rhymes moon with tune, spoon, and soon.

Doris Day had a hit with a recording of the song, featured in the 1953 film, *By the Light of the Silvery Moon*. Fats Waller and Little Richard created R&B versions of the song, and Gene Vincent rocked it up on his album, *Gene Vincent Rocks and the Blue Caps Roll* (1958).

closter, stammel, blitzweed

1. **closter (KLAH-stuhr) (verb):** To break a long-standing record, particularly in a professional sport. New York Yankee shortstop Derek Jeter has joined baseball's elite 3,000 hit club, comprising players who have amassed 3,000 or more hits during their careers. He is still a long way from clostering Pete Rose's all-time record of 4,256 hits.

2. **stammel (STAM-uhl) (noun):** Coarse fabric, dyed red, and used for penitents' undershirts. Nowadays, most penitents just say a bunch of Hail Marys or Our Fathers. However, some monks and nuns wore hairshirts up until the 1960s.

3. **blitzweed (BLITZ-weed) (noun):** The common name given to a type of weed used to cover areas in England devastated by bombing during World War II. Germany's sustained bombing of England, called the Blitz, lasted from September 7, 1940 to May 10, 1941.

The fake word is:
closter

In 1919, no one could believe that anyone would ever beat the home run record set in 1884 by Ned Williamson of the Chicago White Stockings (which later became known as the Chicago Cubs). He had hit 27 home runs in a single season. The record stood for 35 years.

It was broken in 1919 by a promising left-handed pitcher belonging to the Boston Red Sox. That year, George Herman "Babe" Ruth hit 29 home runs. Ruth's new single-season record was considered unbreakable. The next year, however, it was nearly doubled by an outfielder for the New York Yankees. The recently traded Babe Ruth hit 54 home runs in 1920. Seven years later, Ruth beat his record again, with 60 home runs. That record stood until it was broken in 1961 by another Yankee, Roger Maris.

Hit the Sack(cloth)

A hair shirt (sometimes written as one word) was a coarse garment, typically made of goats' hair, that the faithful would wear while performing penance. A hair shirt is extremely uncomfortable, especially when worn around one's loins, a not uncommon practice in the good old days. By wearing the garment, penitents were reminded of their naughtiness while itching like crazy. At other times, a hair shirt was worn during mourning.

About the Author

William Wilson is a high school English teacher in High Point, North Carolina. He lives in nearby Winston-Salem with his family.

DAILY BENDER

Want Some More?

Hit up our humor blog, The Daily Bender, to get your fill of all things funny—be it subversive, odd, offbeat, or just plain mean. The Bender editors are there to get you through the day and on your way to happy hour. Whether we're linking to the latest video that made us laugh or calling out (or bullshit on) whatever's happening, we've got what you need for a good laugh.

If you like our book, you'll love our blog. (And if you hated it, "man up" and tell us why.) Visit The Daily Bender for a shot of humor that'll serve you until the bartender can.

Sign up for our newsletter at
www.adamsmedia.com/blog/humor
and download our Top Ten Maxims No Man Should Live Without.